P9-CCV-595

How Grammar Works

A Self-Teaching Guide

Second Edition

Patricia Osborn

John Wiley & Sons, Inc.

New York • Chichester • Weinheim • Brisbane • Singapore • Toronto

This book is printed on acid-free paper. ♾

Copyright © 1989 by John Wiley & Sons, Inc. All rights reserved
Copyright © 1999 by Patricia Osborn

Published by John Wiley & Sons, Inc.
Published simultaneously in Canada

No part of this publication may be reproduced, stored in a retrieval system or
transmitted in any form or by any means, electronic, mechanical, photocopying,
recording, scanning or otherwise, except as permitted under Sections 107 or 108 of
the 1976 United States Copyright Act, without either the prior written permission of
the Publisher, or authorization through payment of the appropriate per-copy fee to
the Copyright Clearance Center, 222 Rosewood Drive, Danvers, MA 01923, (978)
750-8400, fax (978) 750-4744. Requests to the Publisher for permission should be
addressed to the Permissions Department, John Wiley & Sons, Inc., 605 Third
Avenue, New York, NY 10158-0012, (212) 850-6011, fax (212) 850-6008, E-Mail:
PERMREQ @ WILEY.COM.

This publication is designed to provide accurate and authoritative information in
regard to the subject matter covered. It is sold with the understanding that the
publisher is not engaged in rendering professional services. If professional advice or
other expert assistance is required, the services of a competent professional person
should be sought.

ISBN 0-471-24388-4

ACC Library Services
Austin, Texas

Printed in the United States of America

10 9 8 7 6

Contents

II   Action and Interaction: The System at Work

10   Word Order Is Part of Meaning   79

11   Just Enough Punctuation   87

12   The Five Ws and an H   99

13   The Amazing Word *Be* and Its Many Faces   105

14   More about Pronouns and Nouns   117

15   Introducing the Verbals   130

Introduction to Revised Edition

This book is dedicated to helping you attain a firm grasp of the fundamental system of grammar that powers the English language. With such an understanding, you'll find it easier to make the right choices when you speak and write because you'll know what is considered correct and, most important of all, you'll know why.

Grammar is much more than a collection of rules. It's a complete system that functions as a whole and on many levels. *How Grammar Works* takes you through it step by step. It's based on the belief that the subject of grammar should not be rule-bound, humorless business, but approached for what it is: a natural and necessary means toward the goal of using language more advantageously.

In this new edition, you'll find more practice exercises to give you more opportunity to check your understanding of the essential elements of grammar and usage as you go along.

Although grammar is basically a description of how a language works, a person's manner of speaking and writing does matter. Fair or not, you're often judged not only by what you know and do, but by how well you express yourself. Because this is so, this latest edition includes a helpful new chapter, "Making the Right Choices," that explains how to make grammar work for you.

How Grammar Works also highlights the connection of grammar to both writing and reading. It lets you get a feel of good writing and grammar in action, via excerpts from works by world-famous authors from Mark Twain to Toni Morrison. It also stresses how a knowledge of grammar can help you become a better reader.

It's hard to fix something unless you know how it works, and this edition of *How Grammar Works,* like the first, is written to give you the tools that you need speak, write, and read more effectively.

How to Use This Book

This book is designed to guide you step by step through the basics of English grammar. Part I will help you learn to strip a sentence down to its essentials to discover the underlying principles of its grammar. As you work with examples, you will become familiar with the important relationship among the words at work in every sentence that we speak and write.

The opening chapters of Part I progress from the simple to the complex, yet they present fundamentals of grammar that should become even clearer if you review them after finishing the entire section.

Part II takes the concepts that you have mastered and builds from this groundwork. As you work in these chapters, maintain the habit of identifying the key elements of every sentence, a basic skill that gains in importance as sentences become more involved and complex.

You will find three types of exercises in this guide. One is a clear, direct reinforcement of the concept just presented and lets you check your mastery of it. Space is provided for your responses, and correct answers follow so that you can quickly check your work. If you have trouble with one of these exercises, reread the section that precedes it and try again.

The second type of exercise includes excerpts from works of literary merit, chosen to give you practice working with selections from novels, short stories, and nonfiction. You should not expect 100 percent accuracy from yourself with these. Their purpose is to help you become more aware of grammar and the value of its application to material encountered outside of a textbook setting.

The third type of exercise is the self-test that ends most chapters. If you have difficulty with a self-test, reread the points that are unclear, and try again. Don't continue until you have a firm grasp of a chapter's contents, because each new chapter builds on the information in previous ones.

In working with this guide, concentrate on the work that words actually do in sentences, not on grammatical terms and definitions. Grammar goes beyond rules and definitions. It is the study of the system that powers one of our most useful and often-used inventions—language. Understanding grammar can put you more in control of your language and enable you to speak, write, and even read more effectively.

The second half of *How Grammar Works* reveals how the various parts of an English sentence—words, phrases, and clauses—combine and relate in an infinite number of ways. As you go through the exercises, keep in mind the basic concepts learned in the beginning chapters. This understanding will help you use the system of grammar to its best advantage.

Part II also contains a section on usage that will serve as a guideline to making the right choice between words that are often confused and misused. After you have completed the exercises, you will know the answers to questions about correct usage and ways to handle your language more confidently.

This book has been written in the belief that studying grammar will prove both helpful and interesting as you gain increased awareness of the endless possibilities of the English language and the superbly direct system of word order generating its power.

The goal is to make you feel comfortable with grammar and the way words work. It is hoped that *How Grammar Works* will provide the foundation you need to put grammar successfully to work for you.

Sources

Grateful acknowledgment is made to the following:

Page 9: Gerald Durrell, *Golden Bats and Pink Pigeons,* Simon & Schuster, New York, 1977, pp. 127–128.

Page 40: Conrad Richter, *The Trees,* Alfred A. Knopf, New York, 1940; Ohio University Press, Athens, 1991, p. 41.

Page 45: Thor Heyerdahl, *The Ra Expeditions,* Doubleday Publishing, New York, pp. 233–234.

Page 53: Mark Twain, from "The Awful German Language," *A Tramp Abroad,* Harper & Row, New York, pp. 63–64 & 69.

Page 62: Mark and Delia Owens, *Cry of the Kalihari,* Houghton Mifflin, Boston, 1984, pp. 43–44, 46.

Page 68: Zora Neale Hurston, *Their Eyes Were Watching God,* University of Illinois Press, Urbana, 1965, pp. 231–234.

Page 102: Elinor Wylie, "Sea Lullaby," in *Collected Poems of Elinor Wylie,* Alfred A. Knopf, New York, 1932.

Pages 147–148: John Steinbeck, *Of Mice and Men,* Viking Press, New York, 1937, pp. 23–24.

Page 149: James Fenimore Cooper, *The Deerslayer,* New American Library, New York, 1963, p. 312.

Page 149: Toni Morrison, *Paradise,* Alfred A. Knopf, New York, 1998, p. 312.

Pages 176–177: F. Scott Fitzgerald, *The Great Gatsby,* Charles Scribners Sons, New York, 1925, p. 40.

Page 178: Charles Dickens, *Hard Times,* New American Library, New York, pp. 30–31.

Page 178: Robert Claiborne, *Our Marvelous Native Tongue,* Times Books, New York, 1963, p. 181.

Pages 178–179: Daniel J. Boorstin, *The Discoverers,* Random House, New York, 1983, p. 484.

Page 179: Isak Dinesen, *Out of Africa,* Vintage Books, New York, 1972, p. 15.

Page 221: Richard P. Feynman, *Surely You're Joking, Mr. Feynman!,* W. W. Norton, New York, 1985, p. 256.

PART I

THE ESSENTIALS OF LANGUAGE

1 What Is Grammar, Anyway?

Early people invented language, just as human beings have had to invent all of our other tools, from the simple stone axe to the latest technology. Almost all inventions are attempts to improve our quality of life, and language is no different. As the world becomes more complex, the tool of language adapts and changes with it.

No one questions the importance of language. It's very different with grammar.

Grammar is not merely a set of rules to memorize and follow so that you can speak correctly and write better. Grammar is really an analysis of language. Like a technical manual, a guide to English grammar goes beyond the surface to show you the essential parts of our language, how they relate to one another, and how they fit together into sentences. Just as knowledge about the operation of one combustion engine illustrates the principle behind all combustion engines, so a study of grammar teaches you the basic construction of all sentences. Even as they grow more complicated, they still operate on the same principle.

Using language is like driving a car. When you drive, you think about the road, the traffic, and your destination. As you drive along, you don't have to remind your hands to steer or your foot to press the proper pedal. If you did, you'd freeze at the steering wheel. There is too much going on at once.

To a driver, operating a car becomes automatic. It is much the same with language. When you talk, you don't think in terms of grammar. You think about ideas, about what you want to say. Your mind is not on the process but on the goal you want to reach with your words.

You can be a good driver without being able to name the parts of an engine and explain how they work, but knowledge of a car's mechanical system helps you judge its performance and anticipate its response. An engineer can diagram the mechanical system of an automobile to show its parts and their relationship to one another. (See Figure 1-1.)

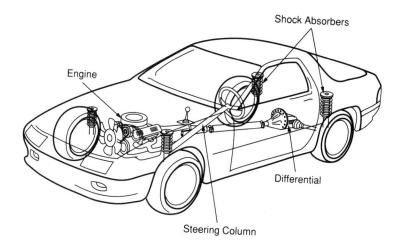

FIGURE 1-1

The clause

A COMPOUND–COMPLEX SENTENCE
    When you check the diagram of a sentence,
you discover the relationship of its parts, and
their function becomes clearer.

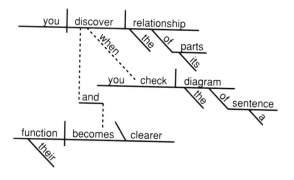

FIGURE 1-2

In the same way, a grammatical diagram shows the parts of a sentence and their relationship to each other. (See Figure 1-2.) Both diagrams serve a similar purpose. When you check the diagram of a sentence, you discover the relationship of its parts, and their function becomes clearer.

Understanding the system that makes English work—its grammar—can help you spot and label problems in your speech and writing, then learn to eliminate them.

A study of grammar provides an inside understanding of language. You learn what the parts of speech are designed to do and why. This discovery enables you to cut through to the core words of a sentence and thus become a more effective reader.

In this way, knowledge of grammar gives you greater control of your language when you read, speak, and write.

2 Nouns: The Building Blocks of Sentences

Because language was invented so long ago, it's at times regarded as something holy or even magic. In fact, from the beginning people have used words not simply as tools but as ways to gain and hold power. In a world without words, early people lived in darkness and fear. They had no way to explain the causes of thunder, fire, sickness, sunsets, and comets.

After the invention of language, some claimed to know the secrets of the universe and the magic spells that would make the gods less angry. Today we think of such beliefs in magic as superstition, but the high priests' and sorcerers' command of language and knowledge gave them power. Primitive people looked up to such men and called them wise.

NOUNS COME FIRST

Babies seem to follow the same steps that early people must have taken to invent a language. Let's look at how a baby begins to use words.

What are among the first words a baby learns?

Mama

Daddy

Baby

cookie

First come the important people or things in a baby's life. Words such as *bowwow* and *ticktock* do not just denote sounds. They are used as naming words for dog and clock because they have a singsong quality that babies like and find easy to imitate.

Tourists in a foreign country also need the names of things first. They want to know how to say *restaurant, menu, ticket, price.*

In the same way, early people must have made up names for *deer, wolf, fire,* or *danger* among the first words in their new invention, language.

Baby Talk Makes Sense

Baby talk shows how you can make yourself understood quite well, even if your language is limited to names of things, called **nouns,** in a study of grammar.

Here are examples of baby talk using only names (nouns). Is there any doubt what Baby is trying to say?

- cookie

- Baby, cookie

- Mama, cookie, Baby

- cookie, floor

The connection isn't clear with other kinds or classes of words, only with nouns (or names). For example, consider these:

- under, concerning, without

- and, since, although

- drive, burn, wash

None of these sets of words seems to have a special sense when taken together as a sentence.

Now, try these nouns:

- baseball, window, lamp

- lightning, barn, fire

- terrorists, airplane, hostages

Is there any question that a definite idea connects the three nouns in each set? What would you add to turn them into complete sentences? You can easily see how nouns (names) are the building blocks of language. Nouns are also a key to understanding when you read.

WHAT IS A NOUN?

A noun belongs to a class of words that name a person, place, action, quality—anything for which people need to invent a name.

Because a noun is a name, it will always answer the questions *who* or *what*.

Who is talking?

a man

Larry

the parrot

an actress

What is your favorite subject?

sports

food

politics

science

What do you want most in life?

freedom

money

success

happiness

Each of the listed words answers the questions *who* or *what*. Each is a noun, even though not all name something solid that you can point to and see. Using this as a basis, grammar classifies nouns into two groups, concrete and abstract. **Concrete nouns** name what can actually be sensed. For example, all of the following underlined words are concrete nouns:

we see a <u>person</u>

we taste <u>food</u>

we hear <u>music</u>

we smell <u>smoke</u>

we feel a <u>shiver</u>

go up our <u>spine</u>

Abstract nouns name qualities not directly sensed. Examples:

freedom

success

pride

happiness

Read the following paragraph and list, in order, the nouns that you find. Remember, a noun is a naming word that answers the question *who* or *what* in a sentence.

The following selection is from a paragraph by naturalist Gerald Durrell in *Golden Bats and Pink Pigeons*. As you read it, don't be surprised if you aren't sure whether some words are nouns. For now, it is important only to get a feeling for nouns and to become aware that naming words—or nouns—is what the selection is really about.

A WORLD OF WONDERS

Any naturalist at certain moments has experienced a thrill at the beauty and complexity of life, and a feeling of depression that one lifetime is an unfairly short span in such a paradise of wonders as the world is. You get this feeling when, for the first time, you see the beauty, variety, and lushness of a tropical rain forest, with its maze of a thousand different trees, each bedecked with garlands of orchids, enmeshed in a web of creepers. There are so many species that you cannot believe that number of different forms have evolved. You feel it when you see for the first time a great congregation of mammals living together or a vast, restless conglomeration of birds. You feel it when you see a butterfly or a dragonfly emerge from its cocoon . . . when you first see a stick or a leaf turn into an insect, or a piece of dappled shade into a herd of zebras. You feel it when you see a gigantic school of dolphins stretching as far as the eye can see, rocking and leaping joyously through their blue world; or a tiny spider manufacturing from its body a transparent, seemingly unending line that will act as a transport as it sets out on its aerial exploration of its world.

Nouns: _____

TIP

Words such as *you* or *they* do not actually name someone or something specific and therefore are not nouns. They are called **pronouns** and take the place of nouns. Pronouns will be covered in chapter 5.

TIP

Identifying nouns can sometimes be tricky because much depends upon how a word works in a sentence.

Compare the following two sentences:
a. The <u>house</u> is large.
b. The house <u>payment</u> is large. What is large? In a, *house* answers the question and is therefore a noun. In b, *payment* is the answer and the noun. In b, *house* answers "What payment?" not "What?"

_____

_____

_____

_____

Answers: 1. naturalist 2. moments 3. thrill 4. beauty 5. complexity 6. life 7. feeling 8. depression 9. lifetime 10. span 11. paradise 12. wonders 13. world 14. feeling 15. time 16. beauty 17. variety 18. lushness 19. forest 20. maze 21. trees 22. garlands 23. orchids 24. web 25. creepers 26. species 27. number 28. forms 29. time 30. congregation 31. mammals 32. conglomeration 33. birds 34. butterfly 35. dragonfly 36. cocoon 37. stick 38. leaf 39. insect 40. piece 41. shade 42. herd 43. zebras 44. school 45. dolphins 46. eye 47. world 48. spider 49. body 50. line 51. transport 52. exploration 53. world

After you have identified the nouns, reread the paragraph. Try to leap from noun to noun, over the connecting words. See how your mind fills in many of the ideas, just as it did with the sample sets of nouns in earlier examples.

Making nouns a main target can help you become a faster, better reader.

USING DETERMINERS TO IDENTIFY NOUNS

Not sure whether a word is a noun? Even though all nouns answer the questions *who* or *what,* a method for double-checking sometimes can come in handy.

The Useful Word The

The little word *the* can do the trick. You can test any would-be noun in a sentence of just four words. Use *the* as the first word and put the supposed noun right after it, as follows.

The _____ is _____ .

Try it with *sky, flattery,* and *under.*

The <u>sky</u> is <u>cloudy</u>.

The <u>flattery</u> is <u>obvious</u>.

The <u>under</u> is <u>small</u>.

The first two examples make sense. *Sky* and *flattery* are nouns. The third is just plain nonsense. *Under* is not a noun.

How Does *The* Work?

The works as a determiner, or indicator, of a noun. This means it's like a signpost that alerts you a noun will follow. Of course, *the* doesn't have to be used every time you use a noun. For example:

- <u>Kittens</u> are cute.

- The <u>kittens</u> are cute.

How do the two examples differ in meaning? As you see, the word *the* not only signals a noun, but carries a special idea as well.

Sometimes other words separate the word *the* from its noun. This makes it even more important as a signal that a noun is coming soon.

- The three small <u>kittens</u> are cute and playful.

1. Which of the underlined words in the following sentences is not a noun?

The <u>volume</u> is loud.

The <u>solution</u> is obvious.

The <u>handy</u> is invisible.

Answer: Handy is not a noun.

2. By using *the* as a determiner, check out the following words to see if they can be used as nouns. Put them in test sentences of four words, as in the examples.

The _____ is _____.

If a word makes sense in your sample sentence, label it as a common or proper noun. If a word does not make sense, leave the space blank.

TIP

The only time *the* doesn't work is with nouns such as *Mr. Jackson* or *Oregon*. In such cases, you must think of the basic type of person, place, or thing being named before you test it with *the*. That is, *Mr. Jackson* is the *man*, and *Oregon* is the *state*. Nouns such as these that name a particular person, place, or thing are called **proper nouns** and should begin with a capital letter.

a. arena _____   b. interview _____   c. belief _____

d. unfair _____   e. peace _____   f. incredible _____

g. creature _____   h. program _____   i. advantage _____

j. revolution _____   k. sugary _____   l. enemy _____

m. opening _____   n. glamorous _____   o. Seattle _____

p. found _____   q. perhaps _____   r. reasonable _____

s. without _____   t. gentle _____   u. matter _____

v. magnetic _____   w. passenger _____   x. menu _____

y. feeling _____   z. Napoleon _____

Answers: Words a, b, c, e, g, h, i, j, l, m, u, w, x, and y can be used as common nouns; words o and z are proper nouns.

Two More Determiners: A *and* An

Like *the,* the words *a* and *an* are signals of a noun. Compare:

- A <u>tree</u> provides shade.
- The <u>tree</u> provides shade.

How are their meanings different? *A* refers to any tree, not a particular tree as *the* does. *An* is used before words beginning with vowels a, e, i, o, and u (such as *airplane, engine, umbrella*) or vowel sounds (such as *hour*) to make them easier to say.

THE SUBJECT: THE KEY TO UNDERSTANDING

- family, vacation, Mexico

It's not hard to see how these three words, all nouns, make sense together. What words would you add to turn them into an ordinary sentence? Here are some possibilities.

- The <u>family</u> spent its <u>vacation</u> in <u>Mexico</u>.
- My <u>family</u> went on a <u>vacation</u> to <u>Mexico</u>.
- Our <u>family</u> took a <u>vacation</u> together and went to <u>Mexico</u>.

As you see, the three sentences say almost the same thing. Nouns alone make the meaning quite obvious. While it's not always this clear, it is true that nouns are the building blocks of a sentence.

One noun has a special job in all three examples. It is the word naming who or what the sentence is about. To find the right one, ask yourself, "Who or what is doing something in this sentence?" Clearly, *family* is the answer.

When labeled as parts of speech, words like *family* are called nouns with reference to the kind of ideas they contain. For example, nouns give people and things names. Nouns can also be identified by their specific use in a sentence.

How Nouns Work as Subjects

Each word has a special function when it's part of a sentence. In all three examples, the word *family* does the same job. It serves as the subject of the sentence. The **subject** is a word that tells *who* or *what* a sentence is about. In this case, the subject is the noun *family*.

Of course, the other two nouns could be the subjects of their own sentences.

- Our <u>vacation</u> lasted three weeks.

- <u>Mexico</u> has something for everyone to do.

It doesn't take a long definition or difficult formula to pick out the subject. You just have to ask yourself a couple of simple questions. To find the subject ask: *Who* or *what* is the sentence about? *Who* or *what* is doing something in the sentence? In the blank space, name the noun that acts as the subject of each of the following sentences.

Subject

1. The clown was wearing a bright orange wig.   _____

2. The group's fans wouldn't stop cheering.   _____

3. A good friend can be trusted.   _____

4. Yolanda is my best friend.   _____

5. The weather forecast promised sunshine for the day of our barbecue.   _____

6. After reviewing the evidence, the jury returned a verdict of not guilty.   _____

7. Without a doubt, Crenshaw deserves credit for quick thinking. _____

Answers: 1. clown 2. fans 3. friend 4. Yolanda 5. forecast 6. jury 7. Crenshaw

SELF-TEST

Check your understanding of nouns by reading the following excerpt from the classic American short story "The Outcast of Poker Flat" by Bret Harte. First, identify the common and proper nouns you find in the selection. Then, list those nouns that are used as subjects.

> As Mr. John Oakhurst, gambler, stepped into the main street of Poker Flat on the morning of the twenty-third of November, 1850, he was conscious of a change in its moral atmosphere from the preceding night. Two or three men, conversing earnestly together, ceased as he approached, and exchanged significant glances. . . .
>
> In point of fact, Poker Flat was "after somebody." It had lately suffered the loss of several thousand dollars, two valuable horses, and a prominent citizen. It was experiencing a spasm of virtuous reaction, quite as lawless and ungovernable as any of the acts that had provoked it. A secret committee had determined to rid the town of all improper persons. This was done permanently in regard of two men who were then hanging from the boughs of a sycamore in the gulch, and temporarily in the banishment of certain other objectionable characters. . . .
>
> Mr. Oakhurst was right in supposing that he was included in this category.

Nouns: _____

_____

_____

Nouns used as subjects: _____

_____

ANSWERS

Nouns: Mr. John Oakhurst, gambler, street, Poker Flat, morning, twenty-third, November, change, atmosphere, night, men, glances, points, fact, Poker Flat, loss, dollars, horses, citizen, spasm, reaction, acts, committee, town, persons, men, boughs, sycamore, gulch, banishment, characters, Mr. Oakhurst, category.
Nouns used as subjects: Mr. John Oakhurst, men, Poker Flat, committee, Mr. Oakhurst. (Note: Other subjects are pronouns.)

3 Verbs: The Energy of Sentences

Standing by themselves, verbs don't carry meaning as solidly as do nouns, the building blocks of a sentence. What kind of sentences would you write using the following two words, both of which are verbs?

- took, went

Here are some possibilities:

- Tom <u>took</u> a taxi and <u>went</u> to the airport.
- Terry <u>took</u> the ball and <u>went</u> for a touchdown.
- Todd <u>took</u> the wrong advice and <u>went</u> bankrupt.

When a set of verbs, rather than a set of nouns, is listed, there's no way to figure out a single idea behind the set that everyone might grasp immediately.

WHAT IS A VERB?

The two essential parts of every good sentence are an actor plus an action. You learned in chapter 2 that the actor in a sentence is called its subject. The part of speech that expresses what action the subject does is called a **verb.**

Verbs can express a lot of action:

- The grasshopper <u>leaped</u>.

Or the act of being:

- The world <u>is</u>.

Or whatever else a subject does, is doing, or did:

- Supper <u>smells</u> delicious.

HOW SUBJECTS AND VERBS WORK TOGETHER

You might think of a verb in electrical terms. The verb is the energy source, which sends out the power that enables the message of a sentence to come through. The subject is what the sentence is about; the verb is what drives it.

What is the secret of being good at grammar? No matter what else you are asked to do, first look for the subject and verb. These will serve as guideposts to help you find your way around in any sentence.

The subject and verb come before everything else in grammar; they alone are the two basic parts to a sentence.

It's like being sure to look for the direction North when you study a map or checking the area code before making a long-distance phone call. Whether it's done consciously or unconsciously, everyone who becomes good at grammar first picks out the subject and verb. When you have a problem understanding something that seems hard to read, it is often helpful to search consciously for these two basic elements. It doesn't pay to ignore the subject and verb; they're really what a sentence is all about.

To find the verb: First, find the subject by asking "Who or what is the sentence about?" Then, name the subject and ask "Did what?" or "Does what?"

Sentences may seem long and complicated at first, but they all can be reduced to these two basic parts.

- Somebody or something (the subject)

- Does something (the verb)

All other words in the sentence radiate from and relate to this core.

You really need just two words to have a perfectly good sentence if one word is the subject and the other its verb:

- <u>Cathy</u> <u>smiled</u>.

- <u>Leaves</u> <u>fell</u>.

- The <u>dog</u> <u>barked</u>. (*The* is a determiner. You can also say "Dogs bark.")

- <u>Maxwell</u> <u>ran</u>.

- The <u>man</u> <u>confessed</u>.

You can add more words to any of the sentences if you wish, but the resulting sentences still boil down to the same two words: the subject and the verb.

For example, read the following sentences. See how the same subjects and verbs are at work both here and in the preceding five short sentences. In spite of all the added words, the actor and the action are the same.

- <u>Cathy</u> <u>smiled</u> at the thought of her plans for an exciting ski trip to Colorado.

- <u>Leaves</u> in colors of gold, russet, and bronze <u>fell</u> from the trees to blanket the ground.

- The ferocious-looking <u>dog</u> in the front yard of the house <u>barked</u> at everyone and everything passing by.

- Losing his nerve completely, <u>Maxwell</u> <u>ran</u> at the sight of the hairy creature hiding beneath the bushes.

- The <u>man</u> caught by the police in the convenience store <u>confessed</u> to robbing eight other stores in the past month.

Although you add more words, the facts in the case haven't changed. (The) man confessed.

No matter how long or how difficult a sentence looks, the most important words are always these two items:

- The Main Subject: Who or what the sentence is about

- The Main Verb: What the subject did or does

After you pick out the subject and verb, read them together. If you picked out the right ones, they will make sense. They will either form a perfectly good sentence or need only one other word to complete their meaning.

Identify the subjects and verbs that form the core of the following sentences.

	Subject	Verb
1. More passengers crammed into the crowded subway car.	_____	_____
2. Most members of the park board disagreed with the chairperson's proposal.	_____	_____
3. In her speech, the candidate for mayor promised not to increase taxes.	_____	_____
4. The sudden noise in the hallway startled everyone in the room.	_____	_____

TIP

1. Such words as *no, never, always,* and *really* are never part of the verb.
2. A verb form with *to* in front of it is never part of the subject + verb. Example:
He likes to go.
Subject: He
Verb: likes
To go is not a verb, but an infinitive, a form discussed in chapter 15.

5. Surprisingly few experts correctly predicted the outcome of the election.   _____ _____

6. The player hurtled over the goal line for the winning touchdown.   _____ _____

7. Without a moment's hesitation, Jensen leaped into the raging waters.   _____ _____

Answers: 1. passengers/crammed 2. members/disagreed 3. candidate/promised 4. noise/startled 5. experts/predicted 6. player/hurtled 7. Jensen/leaped

TENSE: HOW VERBS TELL TIME

What's the difference between *run* and *walk?* The question is not so silly as it seems at first glance. True, they have different definitions, as the dictionary proves. Yet in grammar, there is no difference in their use in sentences. Both can work as verbs.

But what's the difference between *walk* and *walked?* Between *run* and *ran?* Along with its dictionary meaning, every verb carries other ideas that we grasp instantly because of the form, endings, and helping words it takes. This fact makes verbs both the hardest working and the most complicated part of speech in the English language.

To help express these ideas, every verb has three principal parts.

Alone or with helpers, these parts carry a sense of time, **tense,** along with the action or act of being that they express. The first two principal parts, the **present** and the **past,** are used to form the **primary tenses:**

PRESENT: Today, I <u>call</u>.

PAST: Yesterday, I <u> called</u>.

FUTURE: Tomorrow, I <u>will call</u>.

The third principal part, called the **past participle,** is used with a helping verb to form the three **perfect tenses:**

PRESENT PERFECT: Before now, I <u>have called</u>.

PAST PERFECT: In the past, I <u>had called</u>.

FUTURE PERFECT: By some future date, I <u>will have called</u>.

Why are the perfect tenses called "perfect?" Anything perfect is complete, and the perfect tenses stress an action at its completion. Here's an example of both the present perfect tense and the word *perfect* at work as a verb.

- The mad scientist <u>has perfected</u> a formula for turning himself into a dragonfly.

REGULAR VERBS

The three principal parts of *call* are *call, called, called*. Yes, although it's not true of all verbs, the second and third parts are exactly alike; therefore, it belongs to the class of regular verbs.

Regular verbs add *-ed* to their basic forms. Here are some examples:

aim	aimed	aimed
laugh	laughed	laughed
smell	smelled	smelled
play	played	played
walk	walked	walked

If a verb is regular, the dictionary does not show how to form its other principal parts. It's taken for granted that you'll add *-ed*.

Some *-ed* verbs vary slightly. Many use the same *-ed* sound but need a change in spelling to make them easier to pronounce correctly. These include such verbs as:

try	tried	tried
cry	cried	cried
phone	phoned	phoned
vote	voted	voted
drop	dropped	dropped
nod	nodded	nodded

Since such variant spellings can cause problems, the dictionary helps by listing all parts of verbs such as these.

IRREGULAR VERBS

Forming primary and perfect tense with regular verbs is easy. In fact, it's so easy that it seems foolish to say there are second and third parts when they are the same. The difficulty comes when you meet the irregular verbs, which frequently have second and third parts that differ.

First, check out the three principal parts of a few of them.

go	went	gone
do	did	done
sink	sank	sunk
think	thought	thought
ring	rang	rung
sing	sang	sung
bring	brought	brought
teach	taught	taught

Why isn't it "bring, brang, brung?" Or "teach, teached, teached?" Or, for that matter, "reach, raught, raught?" A look at the differences among a few irregular verbs tells the story. Today's English is a juicy stew of words that have been adopted from various languages at various times. Many such verbs are so common in English that we hardly notice how irregular they are.

The importance of knowing the three principal parts becomes clear when you chart the tenses of irregular verbs.

Primary Tenses:

PRESENT:	Today, I <u>go</u>.	I <u>write</u>.
PAST:	Yesterday I <u>went</u>.	I <u>wrote</u>.
FUTURE:	Tomorrow, I <u>will go</u>.	I <u>will write</u>.

Perfect Tenses:

PRESENT PERFECT:	I <u>have gone</u>.	I <u>have written</u>.
PAST PERFECT:	I <u>had gone</u>.	I <u>had written</u>.
FUTURE PERFECT:	I <u>will have gone</u>.	I <u>will have written</u>.

TIP

Helpers such as *will, have, had* and *will have* constitute an important part of the verb. When identifying the main verb in a sentence, always include the base word plus all of its helpers.

Name the three principal parts of the following verbs. Remember, the fact that two base verbs sound alike doesn't mean that they follow the same pattern. If you aren't careful, reciting principal parts of verbs turns into a singsong chant, which results in some silly-sounding mistakes.

	Present	Past	Past Participle
1. break	_____	_____	_____
2. build	_____	_____	_____
3. buy	_____	_____	_____
4. catch	_____	_____	_____
5. drive	_____	_____	_____
6. eat	_____	_____	_____
7. fly	_____	_____	_____
8. grow	_____	_____	_____
9. leave	_____	_____	_____
10. make	_____	_____	_____
11. put	_____	_____	_____
12. rise	_____	_____	_____
13. run	_____	_____	_____
14. say	_____	_____	_____
15. take	_____	_____	_____

Answers: 1. break, broke, broken 2. build, built, built 3. buy, bought, bought 4. catch, caught, caught 5. drive, drove, driven 6. eat, ate, eaten 7. fly, flew, flown 8. grow, grew, grown 9. leave, left, left 10. make, made, made 11. put, put, put 12. rise, rose, risen 13. run, ran, run 14. say, said, said 15. take, took, taken

---

DO YOU USE GOOD GRAMMAR?

To get credit for knowing good grammar, be careful about choosing the right principal part of the verb when you speak or write. For example, say "You did well" or "You have done well." Don't use the past participle to express the simple past tense or vice versa. This is one of the misuses that may make people think someone "doesn't know grammar" or "sounds uneducated."

Just as important, try not to use verb forms that aren't in the dictionary, such as "brung" in place of brought, "knowed" for knew, "busted" for burst, and "drug" for dragged.

HELPING VERBS

Each of the following sentences use a form of the word *go,* but helping verbs give a different sense to each version.

I <u>may</u> go. I <u>can</u> go.

I <u>might have</u> gone. I <u>should have</u> gone.

I <u>would have been</u> gone. I <u>must</u> go. I <u>do</u> go. I <u>did</u> go.

Also called **auxiliary verbs, helping verbs** used in a sentence are an essential part of the whole. Be sure to include them along with the "action" form, which always comes last in a verb string. Notice how a single complete verb can be just one word (*go*), or can have as many as four different words included in its string, as in *would have been gone.*

Helping verbs help express

Tense:	will, have, has, had, have been, had been, will have been
Possibility:	may, can, could, would, should, might
Ongoing action:	am, is, are, was, were
Emphasis:	do, does, did

From the choices in parentheses, pick the one that best fits the sense of each sentence. Underline all helpers. Remember that the helping verbs (*have, has, had,* and *will have*) call for the third principal part of the verb, the past participle, to form the perfect tenses.

1. The lake has _____ over early this year. (freeze, froze, frozen)

2. Soon we will _____ to see the results of our work. (begin, began, begun)

3. Lars might have _____ if you had asked him earlier. (go, went, gone)

4. The house was _____ of the finest materials. (build, built, built)

5. The person ahead of me _____ the piece of cake I wanted. (choose, chose, chosen)

6. The strong wind had _____ the tree limb down. (blow, blew, blown)

7. I don't know what I would have _____ without you help. (do, did, done)

8. Did you _____ the changes in the work schedule? (see, saw, seen)

9. Last night, Jennie's friends _____ a surprise party for her. (throw, threw, thrown)

10. Vacations can often _____ one a new outlook on life. (give, gave, given)

11. The battered old car had _____ many miles of travel. (see, saw, seen)

12. After the race, Chet _____ thirstily from the thermos. (drink, drank, drunk)

13. The large crate must have _____ onto the roadway from a truck. (fall, fell, fallen)

14. I often _____ to the Auto Show. I first _____ five years ago, and I have _____ every year since. (come, came, come)

15. If angry words had not been _____, the two would still be friends. (speak, spoke, spoken)

Answers: 1. <u>has</u> frozen 2. <u>will</u> begin 3. <u>might have</u> gone 4. <u>was</u> built 5. chose 6. <u>had</u> blown 7. <u>would have</u> done 8. <u>did</u> see 9. threw 10. <u>can</u> give 11. <u>had</u> seen 12. drank 13. <u>have</u> fallen 14. come, came, <u>have</u> come 15. <u>had been</u> spoken

---

HELPING VERBS

You have already seen how helping verbs work in the future and perfect tenses. You'll learn other uses in later chapters.

Some verbs can serve as both auxiliary verbs and main verbs. For example:

Glen <u>has</u> the map.

Iris <u>did</u> the artwork.

And these can have their own helpers:

Glen <u>does have</u> the map.

Iris <u>has done</u> the artwork.

Pick out the complete verb in each of the following sentences. Be sure to include all of its parts, including its helpers. Keep in mind that the main verb can be just one word or more than one word.

1. The proceeds from the fund drive should have been counted by now.

2. After all of her worries, Leslie was happy to pass the bar examination on her very first try.

3. Sometimes a person's eyes will glow red in a color flash photograph.

4. Virtual reality can provide lifelike experiences as a cure for phobias such as fear of heights.

5. In spite of technology, meteorologists' forecasts often do go wrong.

6. Most people would have been glad for an offer like that.

7. Without a doubt, Fran has had an incredible streak of good luck lately.

Verbs: 1. _____   2. _____

3. _____   4. _____

5. _____   6. _____

7. _____

Answers: 1. should have been counted 2. was 3. will glow 4. can provide 5. do go 6. would have been 7. has had

HOW VERBS AGREE WITH THEIR SUBJECTS

Every verb needs a subject, and although verbs work almost the same way with any subject, there is one exception. It's an important one, apparent in both the present and present perfect tenses.

Here's an example of how a change of subject affects the form of a verb.

PRESENT: I talk.

Tracee talks. She talks.

PRESENT PERFECT: I <u>have talked</u>.

Tracee <u>has talked</u>. She <u>has talked</u>.

This change occurs because verbs agree with their subjects in number. **Number** means either singular or plural.

SINGULAR: referring to a single thing, such as box, baby, corner, gorilla.

PLURAL: referring to two or more things, such as boxes, babies, corners, gorillas.

In the present tense, the verb takes a final -s or -es when the subject is a singular noun or *he, she,* or *it.* In the present perfect tense, when the subject is a singular noun or *he, she,* or *it,* the verb takes the helping verb *has,* which ends in -s, instead of have. Compare the following:

- Present Tense

    Singular subjects except *I* and *you:*

    A customer <u>calls</u>. Duty <u>calls</u>. He, she, or it <u>calls</u>.

    Plural subjects, along with *I* and *you.*

    Customers <u>call</u>. Duties <u>call</u>. You <u>call</u>. We <u>call</u>. They <u>call</u>.

- Present Perfect Tense

    Singular subjects except *I* and *you:*

    A customer <u>has called</u>. Duty <u>has called</u>. He, she, or it <u>has called</u>.

    Plural subjects, along with *I* and *you:*

    Customers <u>have called</u>. Duties <u>have called</u>. I <u>have called</u>. You <u>have called</u>. We <u>have called</u>. They <u>have called</u>.

Most babies learn how verbs agree, just by listening. At first they say:

"Baby <u>want</u> cookie."

Then they learn:

"I <u>want</u> a cookie. Daddy <u>loves</u> Baby."

"He <u>loves</u> Baby. The baby <u>wants</u> a cookie."

Note: Special points about agreement of subjects and verbs will be discussed in later chapters.

SELF-TEST

List the second and third principal parts (past and past participle) of the following verbs. Decide whether each is regular, ending in *-ed* and *-d,* or irregular. Check a dictionary if you are unsure.

	Past	Past Participle		Past	Past Participle
1. list	_____	_____	2. see	_____	_____
3. taste	_____	_____	4. come	_____	_____
5. take	_____	_____	6. express	_____	_____
7. give	_____	_____	8. spend	_____	_____
9. forget	_____	_____	10. wear	_____	_____
11. call	_____	_____	12. buy	_____	_____
13. try	_____	_____	14. expect	_____	_____
15. choose	_____	_____			

ANSWERS

1. listed, listed 2. saw, seen 3. tasted, tasted 4. came, come 5. took, taken 6. expressed, expressed 7. gave, given 8. spent, spent 9. forgot, forgotten 10. wore, worn 11. called, called 12. bought, bought 13. tried, tried 14. expected, expected 15. chose, chosen

List the correct choice of verb form from those in parentheses. Remember the need for choosing the right principal part and for subject/verb agreement.

1. In the 20th century many advances (was made, were made) in the fields of science and technology. _____

2. Henry Ford (builded, built) the first inexpensive automobile that put America on wheels. _____

3. The Wright brothers had (flew, flied, flown) the first airplane in 1903. _____

4. Just 24 years later, the first nonstop transatlantic flight (was taken, was took) by Charles Lindbergh. _____

5. Sigmund Freud (brang, brought, brung) psychoanalysis to attention as a treatment for mental problems. _____

6. Computer science (had did, has done) much to revolutionize communication. _____

7. Charles Babbage (is knowed, is known) as the designer of the first modern computer. _____

8. Countless people (has took, has taken, have took, have taken) part in its development since. _____

9. Innumerable astronauts (have gone, have went) into space. _____
_____

10. Yet not enough (has been did, has been done) to cure our social problems here on Earth. _____

ANSWERS

1. were made 2. built 3. flown 4. was taken 5. brought 6. has done 7. is known 8. have taken 9. have gone 10. has been done

4 Complements: The Completion of the Verb

Verbs are the part of speech that makes sentences go. They show the action of the subject and express tense, or relative time: past, present, or future.

Some sentences are complete in themselves with just a subject and a verb.

- An eagle soars.

- The sun has risen.

- Our side will win.

The pattern of these sentences is Actor (Subject) + Action (Verb).

Some verbs carry action from the subject to a goal. The subjects and verbs of these sentences leave you up in the air. They need an additional word to answer the questions *who* or *what*. For example:

Terry hit _____

Stan saw _____

Cassie made _____

These actor + action combinations don't make complete sense without a word to fill in the blank. That word is called a **complement** because it completes the meaning of the verb.

Terry hit (who or what?)   Stan saw (who or what?)

    the target?   the movie?

    his elbow?   Kathy?

    the jackpot?   the light?

In the blank space goes a word to answer the question *who* or *what*. The pattern for such a sentence is

Actor + Action → Goal (Subject + Verb → Complement)

FINDING THE COMPLEMENT

To identify the complement, just follow these three steps.

1. Find the subject (S).

2. Find the verb (V), including its helpers.

3. Name the subject and verb, then ask *who* or *what*. The answer will be the complement (C) if the sentence has one.

There are two types of complements: direct objects and subjective complements.

Direct Objects

In a sentence such as "Terry hit the jackpot," the verb *hit* carries the action across from the subject, *Terry,* to its complement, *jackpot.* Because it receives the action, a word used as this kind of complement is called a **direct object.**

As used here, *hit* is called a **transitive verb,** from the Latin root *trans-,* meaning "across." A transitive verb carries the action from the subject <u>across</u> to an object. You find the same sense of <u>across</u> in other words, such as *transport, transfer,* and *transatlantic.*

But not all verbs take direct objects. Those that don't are **intransitive verbs.** The *in-* means that they do not carry action to a complement. The pattern for a sentence with an intransitive verb is:

Actor + Action (Subject + Verb)

Some verbs can be either transitive or intransitive, depending on their use in a sentence. Consider the following:

- Charlie <u>burned</u> the bacon. (transitive)
  The bonfire <u>burned</u>. (intransitive)

- The soloist <u>played</u> the flute. (transitive)
  Chipmunks <u>play</u>. (intransitive)

• The puppy <u>burst</u> the balloon. (transitive)
The bubble <u>burst</u>. (intransitive)

TIP

Whether a verb is regular or irregular has no effect on its being transitive or intransitive.

By writing or thinking of short sample sentences, decide which of the following are transitive verbs, which are intransitive, and which can be used either transitively or intransitively.

1. built _____   **2.** grow _____

3. rise _____   **4.** buy _____

5. say _____   **6.** make _____

7. sleep _____   **8.** is _____

9. whistle _____   **10.** know _____

Answers: 1. built, trans. 2. grow, trans. or intrans. 3. rise, intrans. 4. buy, trans. or intrans. 5. say, trans. 6. make, trans. 7. sleep, intrans. except in "slept a good sleep" 8. is, intrans. 9. whistle, trans. or intrans. 10. know, trans. or intrans.

Subjective Complements

Consider the following subjects and verbs:

Lisa became _____

The play seemed _____

Andrew is _____

Each sentence lacks a word to complete its meaning. Each needs a complement.

Notice the kinds of words that fit the blank spaces and complete the meaning of each sentence.

Lisa → a scientist

The play → long

Andrew → a grandfather

None of these three complements receive the action of the verb as a direct object. Instead, they either rename or describe the subject. Therefore, they are called **subjective complements,** and the verbs acting with them are called **linking verbs.**

Example:

> After a few minutes, the woman beside me on the bus took a sandwich out of her briefcase.

Subject (S) = [the] woman

[the] woman did what? took

Verb (V) = took (transitive)

[the] woman took who or what? sandwich

Complement (C) = [a] sandwich

Subject-Verb-Complement (S-V-C) = woman/took/sandwich

The rest of the words in the sentence give you the details, but to understand grammar and to be a good reader, you should be able to identify the main words of every sentence: Subject + Verb + Complement (if any).

List the S-V-C or S-V of the three sample sentences below.

1. Without wasting any time, Laird threw the crudely wrapped, ticking box into the river. (S-V-C or S-V) _____

2. Everyone in the audience screamed at the sudden appearance of the menacing figure. (S-V-C or S-V) _____

3. Because of her helpful manner, Marcia has become a favorite with all the company's customers. (S-V-C or S-V) _____

Answers: 1. (S-V-C) Laird/threw/box. 2. (S-V) Everyone/screamed 3. (S-V-C) Marcia/ has become/favorite

First, list the subject and verb plus the complement, if any, in the following sentences. Then identify the type of verb (transitive, intransitive, or linking) and the type of complement (direct object or subjective complement), if any.

1. Fires in the western regions of the United States destroy many valuable forests every year.

---

2. The famous and talented artist exactly captured the expression of his subject.

_____

_____

3. The limousine to the airport should arrive at the hotel in forty minutes.

_____

_____

4. Each circus clown wears a distinctive disguise especially his own.

_____

_____

5. Within a short time the improvement in Blair's ability to speak French has become evident to everyone.

_____

_____

Answers: 1. (S-V-C) Fires/destroy/forests; transitive, direct object 2. (S-V-C) artist/captured/expression; transitive, direct object 3. (S-V) limousine/should arrive; intransitive 4. (S-V-C) clown/wears/disguise; transitive, direct object 5. (S-V-C) improvement/has become/evident; linking, subjective complement

---

WHAT MAKES UP COMPLETE SUBJECTS AND PREDICATES

- The colorful poster adds a touch of brightness to the room.
  (S-V-C) [The] poster/adds/[a] touch

To know your way around in a sentence, it's best to find the subject and verb first. Then add the complement, if there is one. Once you find these, it's easy to identify:

- The complete subject: the subject and all of its modifying words and phrases. Here: The colorful poster

- The complete predicate: the word or words that tell what the subject of a sentence or clause did or was doing. It includes the verb plus its complement, if any, with all modifying words and phrases. Here: adds a touch of brightness to the room

Here's how it works with a linking verb.

- The best feature of the car is its low mileage.
  (S-V-C) feature/is/mileage

In this sentence *is* serves as a linking verb and *mileage* is a subjective complement.

Complete subject: The best feature of the car

Complete predicate: is its low mileage

The subjective complement is always included as part of the complete predicate.

SELF-TEST

Draw a slash mark (/) between the complete subject and complete predicate. (Example: Most of the answers/are clear.) Then list the S-V-C or S-V. If the sentence contains a complement, tell whether it is a direct object or subjective complement.

1. Buying from catalogs is a popular method of shopping.

2. The assortment of goods in catalogs ranges from the latest electronics to items exclusively for dogs.

3. Reputable mail order companies provide fast, efficient, and dependable service.

4. Photographs of merchandise show colorful, exciting articles of every kind.

5. The actual article in the delivery box sometimes can be an unpleasant surprise.

6. Genuine miracles cannot be expected to arrive by mail.

7. Be careful about ordering and realistic in your expectations.

S-V-C or S-V   Type of Complement

1. _____   _____

2. _____   _____

3. _____   _____

4. _____   _____

5. _____   _____

6. _____   _____

7. _____   _____

ANSWERS

1. Buying from catalogs/is a popular . . . shopping; (S-V-C) Buying/is/method; subjective complement 2. The assortment . . . catalogs/ranges . . . dogs; (S-V) assortment/ranges 3. Reputable . . . companies/provide . . . service; (S-V-C) companies/provide/service; direct object 4. Photographs of merchandise/show . . . kind; (S-V-C) Photographs/show/articles; direct object 5. The article . . . box/can . . . surprise; (S-V-C) article/can be/surprise; subjective complement 6. Genuine miracles/cannot be . . . mail; (S-V) miracles/cannot be expected 7. [You]/Be careful . . . expectations; (S-V-C) [You]/Be/careful and realistic; subjective complements

5 Pronouns: Getting Personal

He just won eight million dollars in the lottery.

What would you think if someone told you this? Chances are, you'd want to know "Who just won the lottery?" or "What person do you mean?" You're really interested in a noun or a name—the subject, in fact. If instead you had been told "Our boss just won eight million dollars in the lottery," you would have had no doubt about who won.

Pronouns have a useful job in sentences: they take the place of nouns. They save a noun from being repeated too often and also serve when a more exact name or noun is unknown.

SPEAKING PERSONALLY

Personal pronouns are the type of pronoun we use most often. To illustrate their importance, here's a scene showing what a job interview might be like if personal pronouns hadn't been invented. In the human resources office of a TV network, a young woman, Lori Lewis, enters and sits opposite the interviewer.

INTERVIEWER:	What is the name of the person applying for the job?
LORI LEWIS:	The name is Lori Lewis.
INTERVIEWER:	What kind of experience does Lori Lewis have?
LORI LEWIS:	Lori Lewis worked three years at a television station in Pittsburgh, Pennsylvania.
INTERVIEWER:	What position did Lori Lewis have there?
LORI LEWIS:	The position Lori Lewis had was television anchorperson. Would the interviewer like to see Lori Lewis's videotapes?

INTERVIEWER: When can the interviewer see Lori Lewis's tapes?

LORI LEWIS: Lori Lewis has the tapes with Lori Lewis. Lori Lewis also has a letter of recommendation from Lori Lewis's former boss, Marvin Mercer. Marvin Mercer is the station manager in Lori Lewis's hometown.

INTERVIEWER: Can Lori Lewis let the interviewer look at the tapes now?

How painful it sounds! If you substitute personal pronouns for nouns in the above dialogue, it will sound more natural and less awkward. You'll discover how often we use personal pronouns and how easy it is to take them for granted. Is there any doubt that our language needs personal pronouns?

HOW PRONOUNS EXPRESS PERSON AND NUMBER

Personal pronouns are easy to chart and worth keeping in your memory as an important language tool. There are three primary categories of personal pronouns:

- First Person
- Second Person
- Third Person

Each of these categories has two subdivisions:

- Singular (one)
- Plural (two or more)

As with most parts of grammar, this organization fits the way people talk and think. First come the three categories in their singular form.

The First Person: I'm Number One

An individual sees the world through only one pair of eyes, and all of us see ourselves as Number One, or the first person. I know only what comes within my orbit. So the first person (singular) is always *I* or one of its other forms: *me, mine,* and *myself.*

The Second Person: You're Number Two

When I am with someone else, that person becomes the second person, whom I think of as and call *you.* The second person (singular) consists of *you* and its related forms, *yours* and *yourself.*

The Third Person: Everyone Else Is Number Three

When you and I talk about someone or something else, we use the third person singular pronouns *he, she,* and *it,* along with their other forms: *him, his,* and *himself; her, hers,* and *herself; it, its,* and *itself.*

Plural Personal Pronouns

When you know the singular pronouns, the plurals are easy.

- First Person Plural: I + you or I + another person or people = *we* (*us, ours, ourselves*)

- Second Person Plural: you + you = *you* (*you, yours, yourselves*)

- Third Person Plural: two or more of he, she, or it = *they* (*them, theirs, themselves*)

(For a more detailed discussion of personal pronouns, see chapter 16.)

PERSONAL PRONOUNS THAT TAKE THE PLACE OF NOUN SUBJECTS OR SUBJECTIVE COMPLEMENTS

	Singular	Plural
First person	I	we
Second person	you	you
Third person	he, she, it	they

THE NEED FOR AGREEMENT

A personal pronoun, as a rule, takes the place of the noun that it agrees with and follows most closely. **Agreement** means a pronoun must match its noun in number (singular or plural) and gender (whether he, she, or it). Of course, the pronoun *I* always means the person speaking, and the pronoun *you* means those spoken to.

In your reading, always know what noun a personal pronoun is replacing. If in doubt, check to make sure.

When you write, make sure you don't confuse your reader about what noun a pronoun stands for.

In grammatical terms, the word a pronoun replaces is called its **antecedent**. Awareness of the relationship between pronouns and antecedents helps you become a better reader and writer.

Examples:

- (poor) I just used my pen to write a check, and now I can't find it. It's unclear whether the speaker has misplaced the check or the pen.

- (better) I can't find my pen, even though I just used it to write a check.

List the personal pronouns and the nouns they replace, their antecedents, in the following sentences. Put a check mark by the sentence that seems unclear.

	Pronoun	Antecedent
1. Jan felt that she must have made a mistake.	_____	_____
2. When Luke tells jokes, they never get laughs because he always fumbles the punch line.	_____ _____	_____ _____
3. Neighbors of Mr. Durham notice that he has mysterious visitors, and they think he may be up to no good.	_____ _____ _____	_____ _____ _____
4. As the blizzard raged, it caused the people in the cabin to wonder if it could stand up against the storm and if they had enough food to last.	_____ _____ _____	_____ _____ _____

5. Knowing Will as they do, his
friends never expected him to be
on time for their surprise party
for him.

Answers: 1. she/Jan 2. they/jokes; he/Luke 3. he/Mr. Durham; they/unclear; he/Mr.
Durham 4. it/blizzard; it/cabin; they/people 5. they/friends/ his/Will; him/Will; their/
friends (_Note:_ His _and_ their _are pronoun forms used as adjectives to show pos-
session._)

PERSONAL PRONOUNS: MAKING THE RIGHT CHOICES

Personal pronouns change form to signal and reinforce how they are
used in a sentence. The following chart shows you the correct forms to
choose. As subjects, use _I, you, he, she, it, we,_ and _they._

> Example: Shelley didn't realize how late it was.
>   <u>She</u> didn't realize . . .

As objects, use _me, you, him, her, it, we,_ and _they._

> Example: Sherie reminded Shelley of the meeting.
>   Sherie reminded <u>her</u> . . .

TIP
Make a note of the forms that are alike and those that differ in the third and fourth categories. Remembering the similarities between _his, hers, its,_ and _their_ can help you avoid making errors in their choice and usage.

To show belonging, when used to modify a noun (often called a **possessive
adjective**), use _my, your, his, her, its, our,_ and _their._

> Example: All of Shelley's friends know of Shelley's forgetfulness.
>   All of <u>her</u> friends know of <u>her</u> forgetfulness.

To show possession when used alone, use _mine, yours, his, hers, its, ours,_
and _theirs._

> Example: Shelley's card arrived a week late.
>   <u>Hers</u> arrived a week late.

As a complement or object, used to reinforce a word previously used,
use _myself, yourself, himself, herself, itself, ourselves, yourselves,_ and
themselves.

> Example: Shelley gets mad at Shelley for losing track of time.
>   Shelley gets mad at <u>herself</u> . . .

SELF-TEST

Read the following paragraphs from Conrad Richter's novel *The Trees,* which tells of the Lucketts, a pioneer family clearing and settling the forest lands of the Ohio Valley. The excerpt takes place after her mother's death has forced Sayward, the eldest daughter, to become caregiver for her four brothers and sisters. In the dialect that Richter uses to capture the flavor of early American speech, Sayward speaks to her brother Wyitt when they encounter the first strangers they have met since settling in the woods.

Read through the selection. Then list each personal pronoun, along with its antecedent. Notice their different uses and forms.

"Well, kain't you say something to that boy?" Sayward had complained to Wyitt.

. . . All he and the stranger boy could do was scowl at each other over the ox's rump. She didn't know what they'd have done without that ox. She tried to scrape up some talk with the boy's pappy but with a woman he was froze stiff as steelyards. Most of the time the Lucketts had to just stand there, first on one leg and then on the other, visiting with their eyes, waiting till a proper time had passed before they took their leave, saving their opinions till they got out of earshot. And when it went too long without a word, she or one of the girls would talk to that ox, running their hands down his soft neck. Oh, he was the most sociable one there, reaching out his snout for the fresh sassafras leaves they picked for him and talking a soft "Mmm-mmmm-mm" deep in his gullet when they would neglect him. The beast's eyes were mild and patient as summer but you could see a world of power lay in his thick neck and the wide flare of his horns.

Pronouns/Antecedents: _____

_____

_____

_____

_____

ANSWERS

1. you/Wyitt 2. he/Wyitt 3. She/Sayward 4. they'd/the family members 5. She/Sayward 6. he/ boy's pappy 7–11. their, they, their, their, they/the Lucketts 12. it/not directly expressed 13. she/ Sayward 14. their/the girls 15. his/ox 16. he/ox 17. his/ox 18. they/Sayward and one of girls 19. him/ox 20. his/ox 21. they/Sayward and girls 22. him/ox 23. you/anyone 24. his/ox 25. his/ ox. (*His* and *their* may be considered predicate adjectives.)

6 Adjectives: The First Add-On

Everyone interested in cars knows what it means to modify an engine. In much the same way, adjectives and adverbs modify words. They don't change the basic meanings; they "soup up," highlight certain qualities, or otherwise affect the words being modified. This is why they are collectively referred to as modifiers.

HOW ADJECTIVES MODIFY

An **adjective** is a word used to modify or describe a noun or a pronoun. Note how the adjectives in the following sentences don't change the action but do change how you react to it.

- The <u>young</u> kicker missed the goal.
- The <u>veteran</u> kicker missed the goal.
- The <u>tense</u> kicker missed the goal.
- The <u>overconfident</u> kicker missed the goal.

Exactly the same thing happened in all four sentences, but a difference in adjectives makes us see an action differently and respond differently, too.

Here are some examples of the differences that adjectives can make without changing the basic meanings of the nouns or pronouns they describe.

- Big or little?
- Green or yellow?
- Friendly or vicious?
- Five or fifty?

HOW TO FIND AN ADJECTIVE

Let these three steps lead you to the adjectives in a sentence.

1.   First and always, know your way around the sentence. Find the Subject-Verb-Complement (S-V-C) or Subject-Verb (S-V).

2.   Identify all other words used as nouns or pronouns in the sentence.

3.   Check for adjectives by determining whether they answer "What one?" about a noun or a pronoun.

Example:
The new movie received good reviews.
(S-V-C) [The] movie/received/reviews.
What movie? The <u>new</u> one
New is an adjective, modifying the noun subject *movie.*
What reviews? <u>Good</u> ones
Good is an adjective, modifying the noun direct object *reviews.*

In English, most adjectives come before the nouns or pronouns they modify, but there are a few exceptions, as the next examples show.

Example:
The path, rough and narrow, challenged us.
(S-V-C) [The] path/challenged/us
What path? The <u>rough</u> one The <u>narrow</u> one
Both *rough* and *narrow* are adjectives, modifying the subject noun *path.*

Of course, the sentence could just as easily have been written, "The rough and narrow path challenged us." However, adjectives are sometimes put after the nouns they modify for special emphasis.

Example:
The hiker carried a heavy knapsack.
(S-V-C) [The] hiker/carried/knapsack
What knapsack? A <u>heavy</u> one
Heavy is an adjective, modifying the noun direct object, *knapsack.* You could also say, "The knapsack is heavy." In this case, *heavy* is still an adjective modifying the noun *knapsack,* but it is now used as a subjective complement, joined to the subject by a linking

verb. It both completes the meaning of the sentence and modifies the subject.

List each adjective in the following sentences, along with the noun it modifies. Hint: First, pick out the S-V-C or S-V, as well as other nouns used in each sentence. Remember that an adjective may at times follow the word it describes and may also follow a linking verb as a subjective complement, which modifies the subject.

1. The runaway balloon landed in a dense part of the Michigan forest.

   _____

2. Dangerous animals like poisonous snakes and carnivorous dinosaurs hold a strange fascination for many people.

   _____

3. The old house, dark and shuttered, reminds me of ghostly tales and possible hauntings.

   _____

4. Some of the greatest literature known was based on actual historical events.

   _____

5. The main course was delicious and the dessert of chocolate pecan pie simply fabulous.

   _____

6. Excessive use of descriptive adjectives is a noticeable weakness of many aspiring writers.

   _____

Answers: 1. (S-V) balloon/landed; nouns: balloon, part, forest; adjectives: runaway, dense, Michigan 2. (S-V-C) animals/hold/fascination; nouns: animals, snakes, dinosaurs, fascination, people; adjectives: dangerous, poisonous, carnivorous, strange, many 3. (S-V-C) house/reminds/me; nouns: house, tales, hauntings; adjectives: old, dark, shuttered, ghostly, possible 4. (S-V) Some/was based; nouns: literature, events; adjectives: greatest, known, actual, historical 5. (S-V-C) course/was/delicious; nouns: course, dessert, pie; adjectives: main, delicious, chocolate, pecan, fabulous 6. (S-V-C) use/is/weakness; nouns: use, adjectives, weakness, writers; adjectives: excessive, descriptive, noticeable, many, aspiring

ADJECTIVE OR NOUN?

Adjective is simply a label given to describe the work a word does in a particular sentence. In English, the same word often can serve as either a noun or an adjective, depending on its use.

Examples:
    The old car needs new tires.
      (S-V-C) [The] car/needs/tires
        Nouns: car, tires; Adjectives: old, new
          What car? The <u>old</u> car
          What tires? <u>new</u> tires
    The car dealer has a discount offer.
      (S-V-C) [The] dealer/has/offer
        Nouns: dealer, offer; Adjectives: car, discount
          What dealer? The <u>car</u> dealer
          What offer? a <u>discount</u> offer

In the second sentence, *car* is used as an adjective, to modify the subject noun *dealer*. In the first example, *car* is used as the noun subject and has its own adjective, *old*.

Pearl and *Florida* work the same two ways in the next pairs of sentences.

- The <u>pearl</u> was exquisite. (noun)
  The <u>pearl</u> necklace was a gift. (adjective)

- <u>Florida</u> attracts tourists. (noun)
  <u>Florida</u> citrus growers dread frost. (adjective)

In the second sentence, both *Florida* and *citrus* are adjectives, modifying the noun *growers*.

ADJECTIVES THAT LIMIT BY NUMBER

- <u>Several</u> critics panned the film.

- <u>Five</u> weeks passed.

- The winner received a <u>million</u> dollars.

Several, five, and *million* are adjectives in the examples above, but note how they can also work as nouns in the following sentences.

- <u>Several</u> refused the invitation.
- <u>Five</u> tried the product.
- A <u>million</u> would cover the debt.

To find adjectives of number, some people ask "How many?" instead of "What one or ones?" Use the question that works best for you.

SELF-TEST

Find the adjectives in the following selection from *The Ra Expeditions,* Thor Heyerdahl's account of his voyage across the Atlantic Ocean in a craft made of papyrus reeds. Before listing the adjectives, get to know your way around the selection by identifying the subject nouns and pronouns, verbs, and other nouns in each sentence. Remember to check adjectives by naming the noun and asking "What one?" or "How many?"

Some of the sentences are more complex than those you've worked with so far, so it may be a challenge to find all the adjectives Heyerdahl uses to describe a day when the sea was "full of life."

IN THE CLUTCHES OF THE SEA

Flying fish rained about us. Another moonfish drifted by, large and round and inert. Something invisible engulfed the hook on Georges' fixed fishing rod and made off with the whole line. Before he could pull it in, a hulking great fish swallowed the first, so Georges' catch was a severed fish head. Meanwhile Ra was skimming over the wave ridges at record speed, and we were all disappointed when Norman announced a moderate day's run after taking our noon position. We were being pulled south by a lateral current. In the last twenty-four hours the starboard corner of Ra's stern had sunk so far that the lower crossbeam of the steering gear was always dipping into the waves and acting as a brake. The water was permanently ankle-deep aft and wavetops were constantly washing right up to the crate containing the life raft under the bridge. At every wave the crate shifted and chafed at the ropes holding the papyrus together.

Adjectives: _____

_____

_____

_____

_____

_____

ANSWERS

1. flying 2. Another 3. large 4. round 5. inert 6. invisible 7. Georges' 8. fixed 9. fishing 10. whole 11. hulking 12. great 13. Georges' 14. severed 15. fish 16. wave 17. record 18. disappointed 19. moderate 20. day's 21. our 22. noon 23. lateral 24. last 25. twenty-four 26. starboard 27. Ra's 28. lower 29. steering 30. ankle-deep 31. life 32. every (Note: _Adjective_ is a term used to name the way a word works in a sentence. Some grammarians call words like _Georges'_ and _Ra's_ possessive nouns, although they work like adjectives. It is also correct to list _the,_ the determiner of a noun, as an adjective, as well as _our, containing,_ and _holding._)

7 Adverbs: Add-On Number Two

Like adjectives, adverbs have very specific work to do and answer very specific questions about the words they describe.

Even the name *adverb* (*ad* + *verb*) makes it easy to remember that an **adverb** modifies a verb, just as an adjective modifies a noun or pronoun. In addition, an adverb can also modify an adjective and even another adverb.

The best way to learn about adverbs is by observing them at work.

ADVERBS THAT MODIFY VERBS

What are four characteristics of adverbs that modify verbs? Base your conclusion on those underlined below.

- Time passed <u>quickly</u>.
- The child <u>timidly</u> asked permission.
- They usually arrive <u>early</u>.
- Early settlers <u>determinedly</u> headed west.
- The angry boy broke the window <u>purposely</u>.

Here are four conclusions you might draw:

1. Many adverbs end in *-ly*.

2. They often have a similar adjective form, as in

    quick   quickly

    timid   timidly

usual   usually

determined   determinedly

3. Some -*ly* words can be used as adverbs or adjectives without a change in form. One such word is *early*, which as an adverb modifies the verb *arrive* in the third example, and as an adjective modifies the noun *settlers* in the fourth.

4. Adverbs that modify verbs answer some very specific questions: *When? Where? Why? How?*

passed how?   quickly

asked how?   timidly

arrive when?   early

how often?   usually

headed how?   determinedly

where?   west

broke why? (or how?)   purposely

QUESTIONS ADVERBS ANSWER

Some Adverbs That Answer *When*

then   always

now   never

sometimes   rarely

soon   later

afterward   beforehand

Some Adverbs That Answer *Where*

here   there

near   far

away   close

TIP

Too and *also* are two of the most frequently used adverbs. Both answer the question *how*. Examples: You could *also* list many other adverbs. *Too* can modify adjectives, *too*, as in "This isn't *too* difficult."

Some Adverbs That Answer *How*

sweetly	bitterly
poorly	well
brightly	dully
carefully	hopefully

Some Adverbs That Answer *Why* or *How*

purposely	accidentally
hurtfully	helpfully

ADVERB OR NOUN? ADVERB OR ADJECTIVE?

To find the right answer, just ask the right question.

Because a word can work in more than one way, its use depends upon the sentence. It can be tricky to identify adverbs that we usually think of as nouns or adjectives. In the following pairs of sentences, see how the underlined words first answer *what* as nouns, then answer adverb questions as adverbs, sometimes called **adverbial nouns.**

- Monday begins the week.
  I begin work Monday.

- Tomorrow holds a promise.
  Our guest arrives tomorrow.

- A home becomes a haven.
  He hurried home.

Position in a sentence does not necessarily determine which words adverbs are modifying. In the following examples, notice how the adverbs *always* and *generously* fit in various places.

- The rich man has always given generously to worthy causes.

- The rich man always has given to worthy causes generously.

- The rich man has given generously to worthy causes always.

- Always, the rich man generously has given to worthy causes.

In each of the previous sentences, the subject and verb remain the same: (S-V) man/has given. *Always* answers *when*. *Generously* answers *how*. Both adverbs modify the verb *has given*.

Notice how an adverb sometimes comes between the verb and its helpers. Always be sure to find the entire verb string and avoid including adverbs in it.

ADVERBS ALSO MODIFY ADJECTIVES AND OTHER ADVERBS

Most adverbs are easy to identify. Whether they modify verbs, adjectives, or other adverbs, they answer the adverb questions: *When? Where? Why? How?* Here's how adverbs can modify the adjective *big*:

- He was <u>so</u> big.
- He was <u>really</u> big.
- He was <u>rather</u> big.
- He was <u>quite</u> big.
- He was <u>not</u> big.
- He was <u>terribly</u> big.

Adverbs can also modify other adverbs, as they do below:

- The package arrived <u>too</u> late.
- The package arrived <u>rather</u> late.
- The package arrived <u>very</u> late.
- The package arrived <u>extremely</u> late.

Note: *How, where,* and *why* often work as adverbs themselves.

- <u>Where</u> are you going?
- Please tell me <u>how</u> to send a fax.

Not Is Important

- The message has come.
  Chris has taken the examination.

- The message has <u>not</u> come.
  Chris has <u>not</u> taken the examination.

The little word *not* completely changes the meaning of the second sentence in each pair, but it doesn't change its S-V-C.

(S-V) [The] message/has come
(S-V-C) Chris/has taken/examination

To make a verb negative in the present and past tenses, a verb and the adverb *not* act together in a special way. Notice how helping verbs are necessary when a verb in these tenses takes a negative turn.

(S-V) Most adults read.	Some adults do not read.
	Some adults don't read.
	Some adults cannot read.
	Some adults can't read.
(S-V-C) Kim likes chili.	Kim does not like chili.
	Kim doesn't like chili.
(S-V-C) Don went early.	Don did not go early.
	Don didn't go early.

> **TIP**
>
> When *not* is used with present or past tense verbs, a helping verb is added to express time.

Note that neither the adverb *not* nor its contracted form *n't* should be included in the (S-V-C) string.

(S-V) adults/read; adults/do read; adults/can read.
(S-V-C) Kim/likes chili; Kim/does like/chili.
(S-V) Don went; Don/did go.

Of course, helping verbs can also be used to give emphasis to the positive sense of verbs, as in the following sentence:

Willie does try hard.

Identify the adverbs used in the following sentences. It should help, as always, to pick out the S-V-Cs first.

1. The dog wagged its tail furiously but showed absolutely no interest in actually obeying its master's command.

2. "Come here now or you'll be very sorry," Floyd said gruffly.

3. Still wagging its tail, the little dog apparently thought Floyd was not really serious.

4. "He always comes sooner or later," said Floyd philosophically. "This is only a game."

5. Floyd held out his hand temptingly to show the doggy treat there.

6. Sometimes it's quite difficult to tell which is genuinely the boss, dog or master.

Adverbs: _____

_____

_____

_____

Answers: 1. furiously, absolutely, actually 2. here, now, very, gruffly 3. Still, apparently, not, really, 4. always, sooner, later, philosophically, only 5. out, temptingly, there 6. Sometimes, quite, genuinely.

A WORD ABOUT CAREFUL USAGE

Again and again, you hear sportscasters and coaches make such comments as, "Brodhause is a real great player. He made a real fine tackle there. We look forward to a real good season." How are they using *real?* The real answer is "incorrectly." How great? How fine? How good? In each case *real*, the adjective form, is being asked to modify another adjective and do the work of an adverb. It really should be *really*.

It's too bad, but there are no true adverbs that have the exact meaning of *sorta, kinda, a little,* and *pretty*. Both *sorta* and *kinda* actually consist of two words: *sort of* and *kind of*. Here they are in their traditional uses:

• I like that <u>kind of</u> car.

• Pierce is a trustworthy <u>sort of</u> man.

• The picture is <u>pretty</u>.

In both examples, *kind* and *sort* are nouns that mean variety or class. *Little* and *pretty* are usually adjectives. Words such as *quite, rather,* and *somewhat* are proper in their place, although they do sound somewhat stuffy.

SELF-TEST

You think English grammar is hard? Read what American humorist Mark Twain has to say about German grammar in this excerpt from "The Awful

German Language," a chapter of *A Tramp Abroad,* the story of his walking trip across Europe. Read it first just for enjoyment. Then, list the adverbs and the adverb questions that helped you find them: When? Where? Why? or How?

> . . . A person who has not studied German can form no idea of what a perplexing language it is.
>
> Surely there is not another language that is so slipshod and systemless and so slippery and elusive to the grasp. One is washed about in it hither and thither in the most helpless way and when at last he thinks he has captured a rule which offers firm ground to take a rest on amid the general rage and turmoil of the ten parts of speech, he turns over the page and reads, "Let the pupil make careful note of the following exceptions." He runs his eyes down and finds that there are more exceptions to the rule than instances of it. So overboard again he goes to hunt for another Ararat and find another quicksand. . . .
>
> In German all the Nouns begin with a capital letter. Now that is a good idea, and a good idea in this language is necessarily conspicuous from its lonesomeness. I consider this capitalizing of nouns a good idea because by reason of it you are almost always able to tell a noun the minute you see it. You fall into error occasionally because you mistake the name of a person for the name of a thing and waste a good deal of time trying to dig a meaning out of it. German names almost always do mean something and this helps to deceive the student. I translated a passage one day, which said that "the infuriated tigress broke loose and utterly ate up the unfortunate fir forest" (Tannenwald). When I was girding up my loins to doubt this, I found out that Tannenwald in this instance was a man's name.

Adverbs: _____

_____

_____

_____

_____

_____

ANSWERS

1. not 2. Surely 3. not 4. so 5. so 6. about 7. hither 8. thither 9. most 10. on 11. over 12. down 13. there (optional) 14. So 15. overboard 16. again 17. Now 18. necessarily 19. almost 20. almost 21. occasionally 22. almost 23. always 24 one day (optional, adverbial noun) 25. loose 26. utterly 27. up 28. out (Note: *Out* may also be considered part of a multiple-word verb, *found out.*)

8 Prepositions: Relating One Word to Another

Can we get along without prepositions? Yes, but not very well. Consider the following:

The woman is the manager.

This is a sentence that leads you to ask "What woman?" The woman who is wearing a beige jacket. "What does she manage?" She manages the bank.

One simple sentence can carry all of these ideas:

The woman in the beige jacket is the manager of the bank.

In the sentence above, the word *in* is a preposition that shows the relationship between *woman* and *jacket,* and *of* is a preposition that relates *manager* to *bank*. There are other ways to combine ideas, but using prepositions is often the clearest, handiest, and most direct way.

PREPOSITIONS IN ACTION

Prepositions help to clarify relationships with a minimum of words. A **preposition** is a word that relates a noun or pronoun object to another word in a sentence. Here's how it works with the sample sentence given above.

The woman in the beige jacket is the manager of the bank.

Using the preposition *in* as an example, ask "In what?" or "In whom?" The answer, in this case, is the noun *jacket,* which is therefore the object of the preposition *in*. What does the preposition *in* do? It puts the jacket on the woman, which is a very useful task for a part of speech to perform. All the words from the preposition to its object constitute a **prepositional phrase.** Here it's *in the beige jacket.*

The word *preposition* itself helps explain how a preposition works. *Pre-* indicates that it comes before a noun or pronoun, which is called its object. The purpose of a preposition is to show the place (or position) of its object in relation to some other word in the same sentence. Figure 8-1 illustrates the relationships indicated by some frequently used prepositions.

To discover how prepositions work, experiment with the example below. Vary the sentence by making a variety of appropriate choices from among those given, and see how they change the meaning.

Draw a line _____ the geometrical figure.

Among the possibilities are:

Draw a line <u>above</u> the geometrical figure.

Draw a line <u>below</u> the geometrical figure.

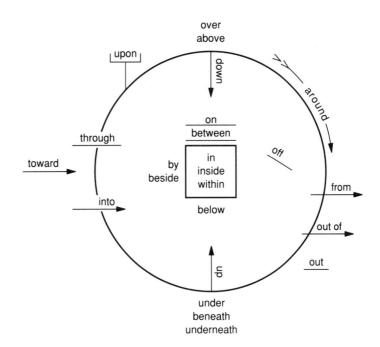

FIGURE 8-1

Write those you choose in the blank spaces below.

Prepositions: ——————— ——————— ——————— ———————

——————— ——————— ——————— ———————

——————— ——————— ——————— ———————

Answers: over, around, through, beside, inside, in, within, under, underneath, beneath, by, upon

See how the underlined prepositions relate their objects to the man.

What man? The man . . .

<u>with</u> brown eyes	<u>in</u> the photo	<u>from</u> Dallas	<u>of</u> her dreams
<u>at</u> the door	<u>aboard</u> ship	<u>behind</u> the plot . . . is Harry!	

How to Identify Prepositions in Sentences

- First, check the Subject-Verb-Complement. Neither subject nor complement will be an object of a preposition.

- Spot possible prepositions, and ask *whom* or *what* after each.

- Every preposition will have a noun or pronoun object included as part of its prepositional phrase.

Example: The cat hid under the bed.
(S-V) [The] cat/hid
Preposition: <u>under</u>
Under whom or what? [<u>the</u>] <u>bed</u>
Prepositional phrase: <u>under the bed</u>

List the S-V-C or S-V, the prepositions, their objects, and prepositional phrases in the following sentences.

1. Guards kept watch around the clock.

2. Inside the hollow tree trunk, a bagful of money was hidden.

3. Through the open window we could feel a fresh breeze.

TIP

Some prepositions consist of more than one word. These include:
because of
in spite of
according to
instead of
as of

	S-V-C or S-V	Preposition	Object of Prep.	Prepositional Phrase
1.	_____	_____	_____	_____
2.	_____	_____	_____	_____
3.	_____	_____	_____	_____

Answers:

S-V-C or S-V	Preposition	Object of Prep.	Prepositional Phrase
1. Guards/kept/watch	around	clock	around the clock
2. bagful/was hidden	inside	trunk	inside the hollow tree trunk
	of	money	of money
3. we/could feel/breeze	through	window	through the open window

HOW WORDS SERVE AS PHRASES

Grammar is similar to a mechanical device. In a machine, a bolt can connect one piece to another. Then the bolt becomes part of a unit, which has a specific function of its own to perform. In a similar way, a word can function as an individual part of speech, and it can also be part of a **phrase,** a group of two or more grammatically related words. Acting as a unit, the phrase also works as a single part of speech in a sentence.

Prepositional Phrases as Adjectives

The following sentence shows how a prepositional phrase can work as an adjective.

> The young man with brown eyes is Harry.
>> What man?
>>> a. the <u>young</u> one
>>> b. the one <u>with brown eyes</u>

The entire prepositional phrase, *with brown eyes,* works as an adjective to modify the noun *man,* just as the one-word adjective *young* does.
Here is another example:

One of my favorite books by Thor Heyerdahl describes his voyage across the Pacific.

(S-V-C)   One/describes/voyage

What one? <u>of my favorite books</u>

What books? <u>by Thor Heyerdahl</u>

What voyage? <u>across the Pacific</u>

As you can see, each prepositional phrase modifies a noun. And one of them, the prepositional phrase *by Thor Heyerdahl,* modifies the noun *books,* which is itself an object in the prepositional phrase before it.

Adjective prepositional phrases usually follow directly after the noun or pronoun they modify, though there are exceptions.

Have you read the book by Thor Heyerdahl about his Pacific adventure?

What book? <u>by Thor Heyerdahl</u>

What Thor Heyerdahl? about his Pacif . . . STOP! That doesn't make sense.

What book? <u>about his Pacific adventure</u>

That's it!

Identify the prepositional phrases that serve as adjectives in the sentences below, along with the nouns and pronouns they modify. It will help to spot each S-V-C first.

1. The best scene in the movie was one near the beginning with loads of laughs.

2. The shrill call of the alarm clock disturbed my dream about a life of leisure in Tahiti.

3. A gaggle of geese is the term for a group of these fowl creatures.

4. The sign upon the post gave a warning about the dangerous condition of the old bridge.

5. A gleam of light through the farmhouse window renewed the hopes of the tired man.

	Adjective Phrase	Modified Word	Adjective Phrase	Modified Word
1.	_____	_____	_____	_____
	_____	_____	_____	_____
2.	_____	_____	_____	_____
	_____	_____	_____	_____
3.	_____	_____	_____	_____
	_____	_____		
4.	_____	_____	_____	_____
	_____	_____	_____	_____
5.	_____	_____	_____	_____
	_____	_____		

Answers: 1. in the movie/scene; near the beginning/one; with loads/one; of laughs/loads 2. of the alarm clock/call; about a life/dream; of leisure/life; in Tahiti/life 3. of geese/gaggle; for a group/term; of these fowl creatures/group 4. upon the post/sign; about the dangerous condition/warning; of the old bridge/condition 5. of light/gleam; through the farmhouse window/light; of the tired man/hope

Prepositional Phrases as Adverbs

Like other adverbs, prepositional phrases can modify verbs, adjectives, and other adverbs. In the following sentences, both prepositional phrases work as adverbs, modifying the verb *go*. As adverbs, prepositional phrases answer the same questions as any other adverb: When? Where? Why? How?

> Many Northerners go to Florida during the winter.
>> Go where? <u>to Florida</u>
>> Go when? <u>during the winter</u>

The five sentences that follow contain twelve prepositional phrases used as adverbs. Identify them and the verbs, adjectives, or adverbs they modify.

1. Until this year, José worked for a Tucson newspaper.

2. After the game, all the fans rushed out of the stadium toward their cars.

3. Airline passengers can put the luggage in the plane's belly, under their seats, or in overhead compartments.

4. People young at heart sometimes succeed because of their optimistic attitudes.

5. The ransom note was written by hand in an almost illegible scrawl.

	Adverb Phrase	Modified Word	Adverb Phrase	Modified Word
1.	_____	_____	_____	_____
2.	_____	_____	_____	_____
	_____	_____		
3.	_____	_____	_____	_____
	_____	_____		
4.	_____	_____	_____	_____
5.	_____	_____	_____	_____

Answers: 1. until this year/worked; for a Tucson newspaper/worked 2. after the game/rushed; out of the stadium/rushed; toward their cars/rushed 3. in the plane's belly/can put; under their seats/can put; in overhead compartments/can put 4. at heart/young; because of their optimistic attitudes/succeed 5. by hand/was written; in an almost illegible scrawl/was written

WHEN IS A PREPOSITION NOT A PREPOSITION?

Remember, a word's use in a sentence determines its part of speech. The following sentences show how the same word can be used as either a preposition or an adverb.

- Brandon went <u>around</u> the world.
  The car spun <u>around</u>.

- Karen worked her way <u>through</u> college.
  Our candidate came <u>through</u>.

- The debate took place <u>on</u> television.
  After the rain, the game went <u>on</u>.
  Leticia turned <u>on</u> the television.

In each case, the underlined word is used in the first example as a preposition and in the second as an adverb. Only the final sentence might be a problem. A change of word order makes it easier to see that *on* is actually an adverb in this example.

- Leticia turned the television <u>on</u>.

- Mrs. Tyler came <u>in</u>. She sat <u>down</u>. She looked <u>up</u>.

In each of these examples the final word is an adverb, not a preposition. Remember that a preposition always has an object. Together, they form a phrase that clarifies the relationship of one word to another in a sentence.

SOME ADVICE ABOUT USAGE

Generations of grammar students were taught never to end a sentence with a preposition. (Or, to break the rule: "Never use a preposition to end a sentence with.") This is a rule more firmly based in Latin grammar than English. Yet, when you know how prepositional phrases work, you can understand why some people remember the old rule and still feel annoyed when they hear a preposition that is separated from its object. Even though it's natural in English to ask "What are you waiting for?" the careful speaker or writer will also know the formal usage: "For what are you waiting?"

- To <u>which</u> magazines do you subscribe?
  rather than
  Which magazines do you subscribe to?

- For <u>whom</u> are you looking?
  rather than
  Who are you looking for?

In each of the next three questions, the final word does no work at all. Since *where* means "to or at what place," and *when* means "at what time," adding *to* or *at* is repetitious.

- Where are you going to?

- When is it at?

- Where is it at?

Avoid expressions such as these. It is correct to say simply:

- Where are you going?

- When is it?

- Where is it?

SELF-TEST

The following selection comes from *Cry of the Kalahari* by Mark and Delia Owens, an American couple who spent seven years studying animals in Africa's Kalahari desert.

First read the passage to discover what it feels like to be in a desert afire when flames engulf their camp. Also, notice how strong, precise verbs power the selection and keep the excitement going, while prepositional phrases add important details.

Then reread the passage and list the prepositional phrases, along with the words they modify. Be sure to choose the right object; sometimes words frequently used as nouns are instead working as adjectives. Make sure your choices are really used as prepositions, not adverbs.

> The morning wore on, the winds blew harder, and the roar from the fire grew louder. More and more ash rained into camp and swirled across the ground in the churning air. By midafternoon, driven by the heavy desert winds, the first flame reached the top of East Dune. It paused for a moment, licking at the tall grasses and lower branches of a tree, then leaped quickly to the top, turning the tree into a thirty-foot torch. Another flame crested the dune, then another. A line of fire invaded the woodlands, and whole trees exploded like flares.
>
> The intense heat created its own wind, a wind that fed oxygen to the flames and spurred them down the dune slopes towards the riverbed at an incredible speed, sweeping them through grass and bush as far north and south as we could see. Nothing could have prepared us for that sight.
>
> . . . After the fire passed us, it marched on across the dune tops into the Kalahari, lighting the night sky like a spectacular sunset. Behind it, the cool pink glow of burned-out trees and logs remained, until the fire's crimson was lost in the blush of dawn.

	Prepositional Phrase	Modified Word		Prepositional Phrase	Modified Word
1.	_____	_____	2.	_____	_____
3.	_____	_____	4.	_____	_____
5.	_____	_____	6.	_____	_____
7.	_____	_____	8.	_____	_____

9. _____ _____   10. _____ _____

11. _____ _____   12. _____ _____

13. _____ _____   14. _____ _____

15. _____ _____   16. _____ _____

17. _____ _____   18. _____ _____

19. _____ _____   20. _____ _____

21. _____ _____   22. _____ _____

23. _____ _____   24. _____ _____

25. _____ _____   26. _____ _____

ANSWERS

1. from the fire—roar; 2. into camp—rained; 3. across the ground—swirled; 4. in the churning air—swirled; 5. by midafternoon—reached; 6. by the heavy desert winds—driven; 7. of East Dune—top; 8. for a moment—paused; 9. at the tall grasses and lower branches—licking; 10. of a tree—branches; 11. to the top—leaped; 12. into a thirty-foot torch—turning; 12. of fire—line; 13. like flares—exploded; 14. to the flames—fed; 15. down the dune slopes—spurred; 16. towards the riverbed—spurred; 17. at an incredible speed—spurred; 18. through grass and bush—sweeping; 19. for that sight—could have prepared; 20. across the dune tops—marched; 21. into the Kalahari—marched; 22. like a spectacular sunset—lighting; 23. behind it—remained; 24. of burned-out trees and logs—glow; 25. in the blush—lost; 26. of dawn—blush.
Adverbs: 1. on; 2. harder; 3. quickly; 4. on.

9 Coordinating Conjunctions: One and One Makes Two

A **conjunction** is a word used to join or connect words, phrases, clauses, or sentences with one another. The word *conjunction* itself offers a clue about how conjunctions work in sentences: *con* (meaning "with") + *junction* = the place where things join or meet.

THE MOST COMMON CONJUNCTION: *AND*

If you can understand the way the word *and* works in a sentence, you'll find it easy to understand how all of the other conjunctions work too. *And* is one of a group called the **coordinating conjunctions,** which connect two equal things.

The word *and* can connect two nouns, two verbs, two adjectives, and so on. In each of the following sentences, identify the parts of speech that the word *and* joins.

- Lions <u>and</u> tigers are native to different continents.

- Diana speaks <u>and</u> reads Spanish.

- The small <u>and</u> agile girl is a remarkable gymnast.

- The flag waved to <u>and</u> fro in the breeze.

Answer: Lions and *tigers* are nouns; *speaks* and *reads,* verbs; *small* and *agile,* adjectives; *to* and *fro,* adverbs.

Now check the following:

- Paul <u>and</u> you are alike in some ways.

Although *Paul* is a noun and *you* is a pronoun, in this sentence both are equal. Why? Both act as subjects of the sentence and share the same verb. Linked together this way, they're called **compound subjects.**

PARTS OF A SENTENCE JOINED BY COORDINATING CONJUNCTIONS ARE CALLED COMPOUND

Sentences may have compound subjects, compound verbs, compound objects of a preposition, and so on. For example:

Minerva and Athena are both names for the goddess of wisdom.

$$(\text{S-V-C}) \left\{ \begin{array}{l} \text{Minerva} \\ \text{[and]} \\ \text{Athena} \end{array} \right\} \text{/are/names}$$

Minerva [*and*] *Athena* is the compound subject.

Connecting Two Equal Phrases

The word *and* can also join equal phrases, such as prepositional phrases or verb phrases.

- Ann searched <u>in the drawer</u> and <u>under the bed</u>.
- You <u>can enter</u> and <u>might win</u>.
- We will <u>go</u> and <u>return</u> on the same day. (Note: <u>will</u> serves as the helper of both underlined words.)
- Some people <u>get an idea in their heads</u> and <u>will not let it go</u>.

In the last sentence, *and* joins two complete predicates. A complete predicate is a verb plus its complement and all of its modifiers.

How to Be Sure What And Joins

First, check what follows the conjunction. Then, compare what comes before the conjunction to find the word, phrase, or clause that matches the other part's usage.

You can <u>try the product</u> and <u>decide for yourself</u>.

Since *decide* is a verb form, you must look for a verb before *and*. That's *try*. (Don't include *can,* which is a helper for both.)

TIP

Avoid using *and* to join words that are being put to different uses in a sentence.
Example: I went shopping and then to a restaurant.
(*Shopping* and *to a restaurant* are not alike.)
Better: I went to the mall and to a restaurant.
I shopped at the mall and then went to the restaurant.

And is like a link in a chain. It connects directly to what's on both sides of it. Because *and* joins equal things, you must check both ways until you find two grammatically equal parts: words, phrases, or clauses that work alike.

In the example, you must include all the words from *try* to *and*. Therefore, *and* must join *try the product* with *decide for yourself*. In the next examples, *and* joins the parts that are underlined. Can you explain why? What is the work of the underlined parts?

- The family went to Nevada and California during their vacation.
- They camped in several national parks and near the ocean.

In the first sentence, *and* joins objects of the preposition, *to*. In the second, *and* joins prepositional phrases. Knowing what *and* joins helps you sort out ideas. It leads to an understanding of how words and ideas work together as parts of a whole.

Connecting Two Sentences or Clauses

A Sentence + A Sentence = A Compound Sentence

- You have done the job well.
  (S-V-C) You/have done/[the] job

- I congratulate you.
  (S-C-V) I/congratulate/you

Each of these is a simple sentence because each has just one S-V-C. Each can also be called an independent clause, because it can stand alone as a sentence. When two independent clauses are joined into one sentence by a coordinating conjunction, that sentence is called a **compound sentence**.

- You have done the job well, and I congratulate you.

TIP

A clause is any group of words having a subject and a verb.

Two or more independent clauses may be joined with *and* or one of the other coordinating conjunctions, which have a similar function. Sometimes the conjunction is omitted, and a semicolon is used instead.

You have done the job well; I congratulate you.

COMPOUND SENTENCES, COMPOUND PARTS

There are many ways to combine two or more equal parts in a sentence. You can write a simple sentence with a compound subject:

The <u>brakes</u> and <u>clutch</u> need adjustments.

(S-V-C) (The) $\begin{Bmatrix} \text{brakes} \\ \text{[and]} \\ \text{clutch} \end{Bmatrix}$ /need/adjustments

Or a simple sentence with a compound predicate:

Mike <u>left early</u> and <u>missed the excitement</u>.

(S-V-C) Mike/ $\begin{Bmatrix} \text{left} \\ \text{[and]} \\ \text{missed} \end{Bmatrix}$ /excitement

Or a compound sentence:

<u>Her victory took courage</u>, and <u>it also required skill</u>.

(S-V-C) $\begin{Bmatrix} \text{Victory/took/courage} \\ \text{[and]} \\ \text{It/required/skill} \end{Bmatrix}$
(S-V-C)

You can even have a compound sentence with independent clauses that have their own compound parts.

Her victory took <u>courage</u> and <u>daring</u>, and it also required <u>skill</u> and great <u>determination</u>.

Notice that a comma goes at the end of the first clause in a compound sentence. A comma is not used when a coordinating conjunction joins other kinds of equal parts, as in the first two examples above.

Using *and* is the first way most of us discover to connect ideas and sentences. Sometimes beginning writers overuse *and* or put compound parts together in a confusing way. Yet the knowledgeable writer can use the same word for telling effects.

In the following passages from her novel *Their Eyes Were Watching God,* Zora Neale Hurston uses language to portray the feelings of simple folk. Here, Hurston describes the coming of a storm on Lake Okeechobee in Florida. List the words, phrases, and clauses that each *and* joins. Simply write the first and last words of exceptionally long phrases and clauses, separated by three dots. (Example: of . . . phrases) The writing looks simple, but you'll discover it's not.

A MONSTER AWAKENS

It was hot and sultry, and Janie left the field and went home.

. . . That night the palm and banana trees began that long distance talk with rain. Several people took fright and packed up and went in to Palm Beach anyway. A thousand buzzards held a flying meet and then went above the clouds and stayed.

. . . Several men collected at Tea Cake's house and sat around stuffing courage into each other's ears. Janie baked a big pan of beans and something she called sweet biscuits and they all managed to be happy enough.

. . . Sometime that night the winds came back. Everything in the world had a strong rattle, sharp and short like Stew Beef vibrating the drum head near the edge with his fingers. By morning Gabriel was playing the deep tones in the center of the drum. So when Janie looked out of her door she saw the drifing mists gathered in the west—that cloud field of the sky—to arm themselves with thunders and march forth against the world. Louder and higher and lower and wider the sound and motion spread, mounting, sinking, darking.

It woke up old Okeechobee and the monster began to roll in his bed. Began to roll and complain like a peevish world on a grumble. The folk in the quarters and the people in the big houses further around the shore heard the big lake and wondered. The people felt uncomfortable but safe because there were the seawalls to chain the senseless monster in his bed. The folks let the people do the thinking. If the castles thought themselves secure, the cabins needn't worry. Their decision was already made as always. Chink up your cracks, shiver in your wet beds, and wait on the mercy of the Lord.

And joins

1. _____ to _____ ; 2. _____ to _____

3. _____ to _____ ; 4. _____ to _____

5. _____ to _____ ; 6. _____ to _____

7. _____ to _____ ; 8. _____ to _____

9. _____ to _____ ; 10. _____ to _____

11. _____ to _____; **12.** _____ to _____

13. _____ to _____; **14.** _____ to _____

15. _____ to _____; **16.** _____ to _____

17. _____ to _____; **18.** _____ to _____

19. _____ to _____; **20.** _____ to _____

21. _____ to _____; **22.** _____ to _____

Answers: 1. hot/sultry 2. It . . . sultry/Janie . . . home 3. left the field/went home 4. palm/banana 5. took fright/packed up 6. packed up/went . . . anyway 7. held . . . meet/then . . . clouds 8. went . . . clouds/stayed 9. collected . . . house/sat . . . ears 10. a big pan of beans/something . . . biscuits 11. Janie baked . . . biscuits/they . . . enough 12. sharp/short 13. arm . . . thunders/march . . . world 14. Louder/higher 15. higher/lower 16. lower/wider 17. sound/motion 18. It woke . . . Okeechobee/the monster . . . bed 19. roll/complain 20. The folk . . . quarters/the people . . . houses 21. heard . . . lake/wondered 22. chink . . . beds/wait on . . . the Lord

Notice how Hurston's use of *and* gives the selection movement, making all of the ideas relatively equal. Ernest Hemingway is another novelist who used the word *and* for a similar effect in his work.

To use language well, you must know how something works, not only to fix it, but also to know how to break the rules effectively.

Compound Parts in a Series

You do not need an *and* to separate every item in a series of words, phases, or clauses.

The store carries athletic gear and exercise equipment and shoes and sportswear.

Instead, use a comma in place of all but the final *and*. The use of a comma before the final *and* is optional. However, be sure to be consistent.

- The store carries athletic gear, exercise equipment, shoes, and sportswear.

- Deer, rabbits, squirrels, pheasants, foxes, bears, buffaloes, and eagles were once plentiful in the American wilderness.

TIP

In using *and*, be sure your meaning is clear.

- I'm asking Bill, Bud, and Ben, and Bruce will ask Bert.

Sometimes it's better to use two simple sentences.

- I'm asking Bill, Bud, and Ben. Bruce will ask Bert.

- Brad's favorite sport is hockey, mine is football, and we both like basketball.

MORE COORDINATING CONJUNCTIONS

You should remember six coordinating conjunctions.

and

or

nor

but

for

yet

All are short; their work in a sentence is not to call attention to themselves but to join two equal parts. Sometimes, as in a series, they can be replaced by commas. Coordinating conjunctions may be divided into two sets, according to how they are most frequently used.

Set A

And, or, and *nor* are freely used to join words, phrases, and clauses. *And* always has a positive sense, *or* expresses a choice, and *nor* is a negative.

- You can choose from blue <u>or</u> red.

- Would you prefer to live on a ranch <u>or</u> in a city apartment?

- I may go, <u>or</u> I may not.

- I have no time <u>nor</u> money to waste.

- We had not slept, <u>nor</u> had we eaten.

Set B

But, for, and *yet,* when used as coordinating conjunctions, usually join independent clauses (or sentences). These three words are just as often seen as other parts of speech.

Here's how they work as conjunctions:

- Elliot's lottery winnings totaled six million dollars, <u>but</u> he kept working.

- Joy missed her plane, <u>for</u> her taxi was stuck in a traffic jam.

- The deal seems promising, <u>yet</u> I would like more details about it.

As a conjunction, each gives a clue about what to expect in the independent clause that follows.

> but: on the other hand
>
> for: seeing that (introducing an explanation)
>
> yet: nevertheless, however

In addition, *but, for,* and *yet* are frequently used as prepositions or adverbs, as in the following examples.

- Everyone <u>but</u> Claire has sent an answer. (preposition)

- I left a message <u>for</u> you on your voice mail. (preposition)

- The plane hasn't landed <u>yet</u>. (adverb)

PAIRED CONJUNCTIONS

Some conjunctions have a partner to signal what's coming and to emphasize their meaning. The five pairs that follow are called **correlative conjunctions.**

- both/and

- not only/but also

- either/or

- neither/nor

- whether/or

The first word of a correlative pair should come just before what is being joined.

- (misplaced) The caller both seemed confused and upset.

- (right) The caller seemed <u>both</u> confused <u>and</u> upset.

In these examples, *and* is used to join the adjectives *confused* and *upset*; therefore, *both* should be placed immediately before the first adjective of the pair.

Compare the following:

- (misplaced) The travel agent both will book your flight and make your hotel reservations.

- (right) The travel agent will <u>both</u> book your flight <u>and</u> make your hotel reservations.

USING PUNCTUATION WITH CONJUNCTIONS

Correct punctuation helps a reader understand the use and meaning of words in sentences more quickly and easily. The following rules can help you punctuate more clearly.

1. When coordinating conjunctions join only two words or phrases, no comma is used.

    - <u>Blue</u> and <u>yellow</u> are primary colors that combine to make green.

    - I plan to be <u>in the office</u> and <u>at work</u> by eight.

2. Use commas to separate three or more items used in a series when all but the final conjunction are omitted.

    - <u>Arizona</u>, <u>New Mexico</u>, and <u>Texas</u> evoke images of the Old West.

3. Punctuate compound sentences by using a comma before the conjunction.

    - <u>The idea sounds strange</u>, but <u>it just might work</u>.

4. A compound sentence of three or more clauses may be punctuated as a series.

    - <u>I came</u>, <u>I saw</u>, and <u>I bought a new computer</u>.

5. With closely related clauses, compound sentences can sometimes be formed without the use of a conjunction; a semicolon takes the place of the comma and conjunction. Each of the following is punctuated correctly.

- The curtain was supposed to rise at eight. The play began an hour late.

- The curtain was supposed to rise at eight, but the play began an hour late.

- The curtain was supposed to rise at eight; the play began an hour late.

6. It is always correct to use a semicolon instead of a conjunction to join two independent clauses, yet a comma will do if they are extremely short and closely related. Both of the following are right.

- I didn't think, I now know better.

- I didn't think; I now know better.

SELF-TEST

1. Read the following simple sentences; list the conjunctions and the words they are joining. Be sure to check the Subject-Verb-Complements, remembering that some will be compound.

   a. The strong wind and driving rain made walking difficult.
   b. Keith mislaid his billfold but found it in his car.
   c. Both Beth and her parents were excited about her appointment to West Point.
   d. You could neither hear nor see well from the back of the room.
   e. The moon and the stars glowed and gleamed like seed pearls against the black velvet sky.

	Conjunction	Words Joined	
a.	_____	_____	to _____
b.	_____	_____	to _____
c.	_____	_____	to _____
d.	_____	_____	to _____
e.	_____	_____	to _____
	_____	_____	to _____

ANSWERS

a. and—the strong wind/driving rain b. but—mislaid his billfold/found it in his car c. both/and—Beth/her parents d. neither/nor—hear/see e. and—the moon/the stars; and—glowed/gleamed

2. Consider the conjunction in parentheses after the first set of clauses. In the blank space, write the number of the simple sentence/independent clause in column 2 that fits with the one in column 1.

_____ a. I know the answers, [for]

1. they tried not to look upset.

_____ b. You must come early, [or]

2. it will be hard to duplicate.

_____ c. The experiment was a success, [but]

3. there was still a quarter to go.

_____ d. Jeff tried to look serious, [for]

4. I studied three hours.

_____ e. I had never seen them before, [nor]

5. did I hope to see them again.

_____ f. They were not expecting visitors, [but]

6. you might not find a seat.

_____ g. We were ahead by two touchdowns, [and]

7. we felt very confident.

_____ h. We were ahead by two touchdowns, [but]

8. his boss did not look in the mood for humor.

ANSWERS

a. 4 b. 6 c. 2 d. 8 e. 5 f. 1 g. 7 h. 3

3. Supply commas where needed. Then name the conjunctions and the elements that are being joined. Some sentences may have more than one compound part.

a. Do you like surprises or would you rather be forewarned?

_____

_____

b. Many people feel a need for more time more money and less work.

_____

_____

c. The witness made a good impression by speaking calmly concisely and clearly.

_____

_____

d. I looked in my pockets on the dresser and under the bed but I couldn't find my keys.

_____

_____

e. We could hardly make sense of his words for he sounded hoarse panicky and almost incoherent.

_____

_____

f. On their trip the Mastersons drove sailed and took trains but they did not fly for they don't like airplanes.

_____

_____

ANSWERS

a. Do you like surprises, or would you rather be forewarned? *Or* joins two sentences. b. Many people feel a need for more time, more money, and less work. *And* joins items in a series. c. The witness made a good impression by speaking calmly, concisely, and clearly. *And* joins adverbs in a series. d. I looked in my pockets, on the dresser, and under the bed, but I couldn't find my keys. *And* joins a series of prepositional phrases; *but* joins simple sentences. e. We could hardly make sense of his words, for he sounded hoarse, panicky, and almost incoherent. *For* joins simple sentences; *and* joins a series of adjectives. f. On their trip the Mastersons drove, sailed, and took trains, but they did not fly, for they don't like airplanes. *And* joins a series of verbs; *but* joins simple sentences; *for* joins simple sentences.

PART **II** **ACTION AND INTERACTION: THE SYSTEM AT WORK**

10 Word Order Is Part of Meaning

> In modern English, [the relationships of words] are expressed through the device of a fixed word order, our principal and indispensable grammatical device.
>
> —*Webster's New World Dictionary*

His the chased tail puppy.

The puppy chased his tail.

His tail chased the puppy.

Anyone who understands English knows that the middle sentence is the normal one. The first is a nonsensical jumble. The last is silly. The three examples stand as proof that English is, at its heart, a language based on word order.

SUBJECTS NATURALLY COME FIRST

The normal order of the English sentence is Subject-Verb or Subject-Verb-Complement. That's why a difficult sentence becomes easier to understand if you first identify these key words.

Unlike English, some languages use endings or inflections at the ends of words to show their use in a sentence. For example, they might add *-um* to indicate a complement and its modifiers. If so, the following sentences would be equally easy to understand.

The puppy chased hisum tailum.

Hisum tailum chased the puppy.

Latin and Greek use such inflections to signal how a word works in a sentence. English most often uses word order or **syntax**.

The natural order of an English sentence is as follows:

Mr. Anderson plodded wearily up the stairs.
(S-V) Mr. Anderson/plodded

There you have it: a perfectly ordinary sentence. You see the subject first; you see what the subject is doing; finally an adverb and prepositional phrase tell you how and where.

Remember, one of the important tasks of language is to create an image in someone's mind. Early forms of written language even used pictograms to transmit such images.

Is this the same sentence as the example above?

Up the stairs plodded Mr. Anderson wearily.
(S-V) Mr. Anderson/plodded

Clearly, it contains the same words, but the reversed order gives you an image of the stairs first. Then you see Mr. Anderson plodding up them wearily. Don't the stairs seem longer this way?

This is called **transposed order,** which means that the S-V has been taken out of its natural order. In transposed order, the verb or part of the predicate comes before the subject.

When you write sentences, avoid using the transposed order just to be different. You might end up confusing someone. You wouldn't want anyone to imagine a tail was chasing a puppy!

IDENTIFYING SENTENCES BY PURPOSE

There are four different categories of sentences: statements, commands, questions, and exclamations. The category depends on the purpose of the sentence, or the type of message the sentence is meant to send. The use of natural or transposed order does much to determine whether we send and receive the intended message clearly.

Statements

Statements are sentences that state, declare, or make known ideas, opinions, or other types of information. Most sentences are statements, and most statements are in natural order.

Example: Jed likes pizza.   (S-V-C) Jed/likes/pizza

List the S-V-C of the following statements, as shown in the example.

1. My uncle's computer needs more memory.

(S-V-C)   _____

2. One of Roy's main problems has always been his laziness.

(S-V-C)   _____

3. In my opinion, Chris should have been promoted instead of Josh.

(S-V-C)   _____

4. Mel might not remember his promise.

(S-V-C)   _____

Answers: 1. (S-V-C) computer/needs/memory 2. (S-V-C) One/has been/laziness
3. (S-V-C) Chris/should have been promoted 4. (S-V-C) Mel/might remember/promise

Commands

Commands are sentences that give direct orders. The subject, which is always *you,* is never included in the clause.

Since the subject *you* is understood to come first, you can consider commands to have a natural order.

Examples: Bring your friends.   (S-V-C) [You] /bring/friends
Do come to the party.   (S-V-C) [You]/do come

List the S-V-C of the following commands, as shown in the examples.

1. Practice your lines for tomorrow's rehearsal.

(S-V-C)   _____

2. Make a habit of being on time.   (S-V-C)   _____

3. Read the instructions carefully.   (S-V-C)   _____

4. Remember the importance of syntax to English.

(S-V-C)   _____

Answers: 1. (S-V-C) [You]/practice/lines 2. (S-V-C) [You]/make/habit 3. (S-V-C) [You]/
read /(the) instructions 4. (S-V-C) [You]/remember/importance

Questions

Questions are sentences that ask for an answer—opinion, information, or another kind of response—and end with a question mark. Part or all of the verb is usually transposed to a position before the subject. (How questions work will be discussed later.)

Example: Did you hear him? (S-V-C) You/did hear/him

List the S-V-C of the following questions, as shown in the example.

1. Can you understand his point of view?

(S-V-C) _____

2. How much time do you spend on the Internet?

(S-V-C) _____

3. What has Edie heard about the new project?

(S-V-C) _____

4. Did Fred appear nervous as the emcee?

(S-V-C) _____

Answers: 1. (S-V-C) you/can understand/point 2. (S-V-C) you/do spend/time 3. (S-V-C) Edie/has heard/ what 4. (S-V-C) Fred/did appear/nervous

Exclamations

Exclamations are sentences that express strong emotion or feeling. To call attention to this, exclamations often start with *How* or *What* and also have the complements placed before the Subject-Verb. All exclamations should end with exclamation points.

Example: How happy we were! (S-V-C) We/were/happy

List the S-V-C of the following exclamations, as shown in the example.

1. What a wonderful time we had! (S-V-C) _____

2. How frightening the old house seemed with the wind rattling the shutters! (S-V-C) _____

3. How clever you are! (S-V-C) _____

4. What a difference your advice made! (S-V-C) _____

Answers: 1. (S-V-C) we/had/time 2. (S-V-C) house/seemed/frightening 3. (S-V-C) you/are/clever 4. (S-V-C) advice/made/difference

HOW CHANGING WORD ORDER CHANGES PURPOSE

There are four basic ways of turning a statement into a question in English. Most require transposing part of the Subject-Verb-Complement.

1. To signal a question, put part or all of the verb before the subject.

Statements	Questions
a. Mike is going to Epcot Center.	a. Is Mike going to Epcot Center?
b. He has been there before.	b. Has he been there before?
c. Everyone was surprised by the verdict.	c. Was everyone surprised by the verdict?

2. Add a helping verb before the subject to form a question.

Statements	Questions
a. Fran speaks Chinese fluently.	a. Can Fran speak Chinese fluently?
b. Kermit likes listening to jazz.	b. Does Kermit like listening to jazz?
c. Many people came to the exhibit.	c. Did many people come to the exhibit?

3. Use an adverb question—*where, when, why,* or *how*—as an opening word.

Statements	Questions
a. Charlene works at the zoo.	a. Where does Charlene work?
b. She finishes work at 5 p.m.	b. When does she finish work?
c. I went to the doctor for a routine checkup.	c. Why did you go to the doctor?
d. Wyman made the journey by dog sled.	d. How did Wyman make the journey?

Note that the form of the question determines the answer. You could also ask, "Does Charlene work at the zoo?" Also, notice how these sentences add a helping verb as an additional sign of a question. In asking and answering questions, pronouns may change too. "How are *you?*" is answered "*I* am fine."

4. *What*, *which*, *who*, and *whom* also introduce questions.

Statements
a. Picasso painted this picture.

b. I bought a new pair of skis.

c. The letter held welcome news.

d. The photographer printed the third pose.

e. Hank chose the convertible instead of the hardtop.

Questions
a. Who painted the picture?
(S-V-C) Who/painted/[the] picture

b. What did you buy?
(S-V-C) you/did buy/what

c. What news did the letter hold?
(S-V-C) [the] letter/did hold/news

d. Which pose did the photographer print?
(S-V-C) [the] photographer/did print/pose

e. Which of the two cars did Hank choose?
(S-V-C) Hank/did choose/which

From the S-V-C you can see that in examples a, b, and e, *who*, *what*, and *which* are used as pronouns. *What* in c and *which* in d are adjectives.

SELF-TEST

1. In the blank space, indicate whether the following are statements, questions, commands, or exclamations. It will be helpful to identify the S-V-C or S-V as well.

   a. You will find the index at the end of a book. _____

   b. How many people will be affected by the law? _____

   c. Give consideration to other people's feelings. _____

d. After a long wait we were finally permitted inside the concert hall. _____

e. How surprised Kay looked about the news! _____

f. What uproar the announcement caused! _____

g. What do you think of the new boss? _____

h. Mail your entry in before July 31. _____

ANSWERS

a. statement; (S-V-C) you/will find/index b. question; (S-V-C) people/will be affected c. command; (S-V-C) [you] give/consideration d. statement; (S-V-C) we/were permitted e. exclamation; (S-V-C) Kay/looked/surprised f. exclamation; (S-V-C) announcement/caused/uproar g. question; (S-V-C) you/do think/what h. command; (S-V-C) [you] mail/entry

2. Rewrite each of the following statements as a question, using one of the changes in word order that signal a question. (Note: More than one correct version is possible for several examples.)

a. Chris has forgotten his promise. _____

b. You can understand his point of view. _____

c. Bonnie will be home tomorrow. _____

d. It cost Ted a lot to repair his car. _____

e. Sarah chose the less expensive CD player. _____

f. The film received rave reviews. _____

ANSWERS

a. Has Chris forgotten his promise? b. Can you understand his point of view? c. When will Bonnie be home? *or* Will Bonnie be home tomorrow? d. Did it cost Ted a lot to repair his car? e. Which CD player did Sarah choose? f. What kind of review did the film receive? *or* Did the film receive rave reviews?

3. Make up an answer to each of the following questions. Remember, a question asked of *you* requires *I* or *we* in its response, and vice versa. (You need not include *yes* or *no*.) Notice the S-V-C of each question, and then write the answer in natural order.

a. Why were you so angry?   _____

b. When do you expect an answer?

_____

c. What kind of music does Wendy like best?

_____

d. Where can I find a good bargain?

_____

e. Whom can I ask for help?

_____

f. Which kind of soft drink do you prefer?

_____

ANSWERS

Many answers are possible.

11 Just Enough Punctuation

A pause, a raising or lowering of the voice, an emphasis, perhaps a bit of body language—these are some of the ways we express attitudes and clarify our meaning when we speak. There's no way to raise an eyebrow in writing, and it's hard to put an inquiring tone of voice into print, so we use punctuation marks to help do this for us. Punctuation marks are simply signals, pointing out how the written language would sound if spoken.

USING END PUNCTUATION

A **sentence** is a group of words that states a complete thought. To show its completeness, a sentence needs a definitely marked beginning and ending. A capital letter marks the beginning, and one of the following three strong marks of punctuation shows the end:

- **Periods** speak matter-of-factly.

- **Question marks** leave you up in the air, don't they?

- How **exclamation points** shout!

Use exclamation points sparingly. Like any other attention-getting device, they tend to lose their power to attract if they are overused. Precise words and careful phrasing will do the job better than noisy punctuation.

Statements

Statements as a rule end with periods. For special emphasis, statements may occasionally end with an exclamation point, but you should avoid overworking them. Here are four examples:

- In times of stress, people can become angry with their loved ones for no apparent reason.

- Why, I am impressed by your store of information. (*Why* is an interjection in this sentence. It has no grammatical relation to the other words, and so doesn't make this a question.)

- I arrived at the box office early, but people already stood in line.

- Esteban asked when the post office closed.

The last example makes a statement about Esteban. It states the question he asked. It can also be called an **indirect question.**

Commands

Commands may end in periods or exclamation marks, depending upon how forcefully the writer wants to make a command.

- Listen to me!

- Please give me your attention.

- Hurry up and get ready. *or* Hurry up and get ready!

- Bring your stereo, and I'll bring my new CD.

Notice that the last example is a compound sentence; the first clause is a command, and the second is a statement.

Questions

Direct questions always end with question marks.

- Does the spaghetti sauce have enough garlic?

- When does the post office close?

- Where will you go, and what will you do?

- Come here, or do I have to come after you?

Notice that the last two examples are compound sentences.

Exclamations

Exclamations always end in exclamation points. Usually beginning with *How* or *What* and written in transposed order, exclamations do not ask questions but are reserved for expressing strong emotion.

- How generous you are!

- Wow! What a great game that was!

- What a wonderful time we had last night!

- How dark it is, and how stormy!

Notice that "it is" is understood in the second part of the last sentence.

Supply the correct end punctuation at the end of each sentence. As always, be aware of the main S-V-C or S-V.

1. What kind of impression did Sandy's presentation make

2. What a good impression Sandy made

3. No lack of self-confidence showed in Sandy's manner

4. If you were asked, what answer would you give

5. If she was nervous, I wasn't aware of it

6. How calm she seemed

7. Realize that someone who looks calm may still be nervous

8. How can you prepare yourself for public speaking

9. Before speaking, know your subject well but don't overprepare

10. You need not enjoy public speaking to do it well

Answers: 1. What kind of impression . . . make? 2. What a good impression . . . made! 3. No lack . . . manner. 4. If you . . . would you give? 5. If she was . . . aware of it. 6. How calm she seemed! 7. Realize that . . . still be nervous. 8. How can you . . . for public speaking? 9. Before speaking . . . don't overprepare. 10. You need . . . to do it well.

PUNCTUATING WITHIN SENTENCES

Using Commas to Avoid Confusion

In addition to using correct end punctuation, it's also important to make careful use of commas to clarify your meaning. Here are six rules for separating words and word groups to avoid confusion.

1. Commas separate items in a series.

- Television, radio, periodicals, and the internet are major advertising media.

- The car roared down the street, around the corner, and through the alley at high speed. (Notice that *at high speed* is not part of the series of prepositional phrases, so no comma is needed before it.)

- You get out the chips and relishes, I'll grill the burgers, and we'll soon be ready to eat.

Don't use a comma when only two words or phrases are joined by a coordinating conjunction, as are *chips* and *relish*. However, a comma is usually used between two clauses in a compound sentence.

2. Commas set off words added for identification.

To Identify a Place:
- I was not sure whether Gary meant London, England, or London, Ontario, Canada.

TIP

Use a pair of commas to set off words added for identification when they come in the middle of a sentence.

As with *and* in a series, the comma can be thought of as replacing an omitted word or words in an identification. With those words added: I was not sure whether Gary meant London in England or London in the province of Ontario in Canada.

To Set Off a Date:
- July 2, 1776, is a date every American should remember.
- The concert is set for Friday, October 24.

To Set Off Nouns of Address:
- Mary, have you met Chet?
- This time, Al, you have gone too far!
- Do quit pacing for a moment, Lonnie.

A **noun of address** is simply the name of the person spoken to directly. It has no grammatical connection to a sentence.

To Set Off an Appositive:

- Guy and his father, Greg, look enough alike to be twins.

- Popinjay, my pet Airedale, has very good manners.

- An expert on the psychology of successful executives, Dr. Clive Cleveland, is today's speaker.

- The car, a Stutz Bearcat, is his most prized possession.

A **appositive,** or noun in apposition, renames and identifies the noun it's placed next to, but otherwise has no grammatical connection to a sentence.

TIP

Always be sure to use commas before and after words being set off in the middle of a sentence.

3. Commas should set off parenthetic remarks—words or phrases that interrupt the flow of the sentence and have no direct grammatical connection to the rest.

- I can, of course, see your point of view.

- Ashley, on the contrary, does not accept your theory.

If the interruption is slight, commas are not necessary.

- Although the error was slight, the boss nevertheless decided to redo the presentation.

4. Commas set off the greeting and polite closing words of a letter.

- Dear Mr. Frazier,

- Sincerely,

5. Commas come after introductory phrases to create an attention-getting pause.

- Nevertheless, the experiment was a success.

- Well, you might have told me that sooner.

- Still, there was no reason to be angry about it.

6. One additional [and important] rule for commas: They may be needed and used for clarity, according to the writer's own judgment. Whenever there is strong doubt, it is better to omit a comma than to use it.

- (poor) It is worse, by far, to overuse commas, that, thereby, prove a distraction, instead of a help, to the reader, than to fail, at times, to include them.

- (better) It is worse by far to overuse commas that thereby prove a distraction to the reader than to fail at times to include them.

PUNCTUATION IS ALSO A MATTER OF STYLE

Because of the importance of being consistent, newspapers and magazines have their own style sheets that state rules of punctuation, capitalization, and usage that their writers should follow. These rules vary in detail from publication to publication. A number of standard style books have been published and are readily available. Many dictionaries also have useful sections concerning style.

Punctuating Compound Sentences

When joining two or more independent clauses to form a compound sentence, you should remember these three rules of punctuation:

1. A comma comes before the coordinating conjunction in a compound sentence of two clauses.

    - The truckload of supplies arrived, but some of the packing crates were damaged.
    - You have your opinion, and I have mine.

2. Punctuate compound sentence of two or more clauses like any other series.

    - The mystery was solved, the lost keys were found, and we could finally be on our way.

3. Alone, a semicolon (;) is strong enough to join two independent clauses into a compound sentence. With a "period" above and a "comma" below, a semicolon marks the halfway point in strength between a period and a comma.

    - In the past, a semicolon was used frequently; in the present, it has lost some of its popularity because shorter sentences are now favored.

THREE POSSIBILITIES FOR PUNCTUATING TWO INDEPENDENT CLAUSES

1. I already checked. I have no quarters.

2. I already checked, and I have no quarters.

3. I already checked; I have no quarters.

It's the writer's choice!

Supply the necessary end punctuation and commas for the following sentences.

1. Mark Twain first read the story of Joan of Arc the Maid of Orleans when he was only fifteen

2. Twain called himself the translator of a manuscript by Louis de Conte her secretary

3. Twain writes that Joan of Arc was born January 6 1410 but an encyclopedia lists the date as in doubt

4. Certainly Joan of Arc's secretary would have known her exact birthday and Twain wanted him to be the apparent author

5. Are you familiar with Twain as a humorist satirist and author of such books as *Tom Sawyer Huckleberry Finn* and *The Prince and the Pauper*

6. Joan of Arc was living in the village of Domremy France when a holy voice told her to don male attire go tell the French court of her divine mission and lead France to victory

7. Joan of Arc went from peasant to soldier to heroine and then to condemned witch all in her nineteen short extraordinary years of life

8. She was burnt at the stake on May 30 1431 in Rouen France her conviction was overturned in 1456 and she was canonized as Saint Joan in 1920 nearly 500 years later

9. How remarkable that Twain liked *Joan of Arc* best of all his books

10. Joan of Arc is a symbol of courage faith purity devotion and ultimate triumph that greatly inspired Mark Twain

Answers: 1. Mark Twain first read the story of Joan of Arc, the Maid of Orleans, when he was only fifteen. 2. Twain called himself the translator of a manuscript by Louis de Conte, her secretary. 3. Twain writes that Joan of Arc was born January 6, 1410, but an encyclopedia lists the date as in doubt. 4. Certainly, Joan of Arc's secretary would have known her exact birthday, and Twain wanted him to be the apparent author. 5. Are you familiar with Twain as a humorist, satirist, and author of such books as *Tom Sawyer, Huckleberry Finn,* and *The Prince and the Pauper?* 6. Joan of Arc was living in the village of Domremy, France, when a holy voice told her to don male attire, go tell the French court of her divine mission, and lead France to victory. 7. Joan of Arc went from peasant, to soldier, to heroine, and then to condemned witch, all in her nineteen short, extraordinary years of life. 8. She was burnt at the stake on May 30, 1431, in Rouen, France; her conviction was overturned in 1456, and she was canonized as Saint Joan in 1920, nearly 500 years later. (This can be punctuated as a series of sentences with a comma after France or written as two sentences with a period after France and a capital H.) 9. How remarkable that Twain liked *Joan of Arc* best of all his books! 10. Joan of Arc is a symbol of courage, faith, purity, devotion, and ultimate triumph that greatly inspired Mark Twain.

AVOIDING FRAGMENTS AND RUN-ONS

In the first draft of their writing, people usually think in terms of expressing thoughts and ideas, not of individual sentences and paragraphs. That's why errors such as those that follow slip by so easily.

- When you write. (Fragment) Use punctuation carefully. (Sentence)

Written alone, the three words, "When you write," say little or nothing. It's only when the two parts are put together—joined by a comma, not separated by a period—that they make good sense.

- When you write, use punctuation carefully.

Groups of words, punctuated as a sentence but not actually complete thoughts, are called **fragments.** A fragment may even have a subject and verb, as does the example given. When checking your writing, be sure to read from each beginning capital to the end punctuation to determine whether each segment is complete and correct.

Like fragments, run-on sentences are just a matter of punctuation. Sometimes called a comma splice, they're not a sign of poor thinking. They result from using a comma in place of stronger punctuation, such as a semicolon or period. To help avoid run-on sentences, review the rules for punctuating compound sentences.

- (run-on) Correct punctuation does make a difference, it affects the way someone understands what you write.

- (better) Punctuation does make a difference, for it affects the way someone understands what you write.

Read the following sentences and determine which are fragments, which are run-ons, and which are correct sentences. Rewrite those that contain errors, changing punctuation and adding capital letters and/or conjunctions, if necessary.

1. Winning her chance to compete in the Olympics. Adrian has achieved her lifelong dream.

_____

_____

2. The Olympics are meant to honor individual effort. Not to prove one country better than another.

_____

_____

3. Competing in the upcoming games will be a thrill, taking home a medal is now her goal.

_____

_____

4. Before each Olympics, many cities compete for the honor of hosting the events, even though they don't always make a profit.

_____

_____

Answers: 1. Winning her chance to compete in the Olympics, Adrian has achieved her lifelong dream. 2. The Olympics are meant to honor individual effort, not to prove one country better than another. 3. Competing in the upcoming games will be a thrill; taking home a medal is now her goal. (May also be joined with comma plus conjunction or separated as two sentences) 4. Correct

PUNCTUATION TO USE, BUT NOT OVERUSE

Punctuation should serve as a guide. It indicates pauses, tone, and emphasis. It provides signposts telling how to read a written message.

1. Overused, punctuation can take away rather than add effectiveness.

   • The small boy, there, in the blue T-shirt, with the Disney world logo on it, is sticking his finger, in the cake icing, and licking it off.

   • Do you mean it??? It can't be true!!!! Really?!!??!

2. Parentheses (like these) stop a reader while commas, as here, maintain the flow better. **Parentheses** are used to set off comments added to an already complete thought.

   • They (that is, the words inside the parentheses) often seem an unnecessary afterthought.

   • You must stop, read what's inside, then go back (as if you had been halted by a roadblock) and read again.

3. You can use—but shouldn't overuse—dashes in a similar way.

   • A dash can prove helpful at the end of a sentence—to emphasize its point.

   • Unnecessary dashes—on the other hand—cause a distraction.

   • (better) Unnecessary dashes, on the other hand, cause a distraction.

4. The ellipsis mark consists of three spaced periods [. . .] used to indicate a word or words that have been left out.

   • "When in the course of human events . . . " is the beginning of the Declaration of Independence.

   • Grace said that she told you about . . . , but you already know that, don't you?

SELF-TEST

Rewrite the following, supplying necessary punctuation within and at the end. You may also need to add words to correct a fragment or run-on.

1. Felicia have you ever visited Salem Massachusetts

   _____

   _____

2. What strange remarkable and even horrifying events happened there

   _____

   _____

3. Salem was once a world-famous seaport but it is now of course better known because of its past

   _____

   _____

4. Doesn't it seem hard to believe that twenty people were tried condemned and executed as witches there in 1692

   _____

   _____

5. Nevertheless the story is true, it is also the basis for *The Crucible* a play by Arthur Miller

   _____

   _____

6. Miller's play shows the fear frenzy and mindlessness that can overcome people's objectivity reasonableness and good judgment

   _____

   _____

7. Nathaniel Hawthorne author of *The Scarlet Letter* was born in Salem on July 4 1804

   _____

   _____

8. The Puritans of old Salem found Hester Prynne the main character guilty of adultery, her punishment was to wear a symbol of her sin the scarlet letter A on her bosom

_____

_____

9. Why so many tourists want to visit Salem each year

_____

_____

ANSWERS

1. Felicia, have you ever visited Salem, Massachusetts?

2. What strange, remarkable, and even horrifying events happened there! (Could also be a question.)

3. Salem was once a world-famous seaport, but it is now, of course, better known because of its past.

4. Doesn't it seem hard to believe that twenty people were tried, condemned, and executed as witches there in 1692?

5. Nevertheless the story is true. It is also the basis for _The Crucible,_ a play by Arthur Miller.

6. Miller's play shows the fear, frenzy, and mindlessness that can overcome people's objectivity, reasonableness, and good judgment.

7. Nathaniel Hawthorne, author of _The Scarlet Letter,_ was born in Salem on July 4, 1804.

8. The Puritans of old Salem found Hester Prynne, the main character, guilty of adultery, and her punishment was to wear a symbol of her sin, the scarlet letter A, on her bosom.

9. It's obvious why so many tourists want to visit Salem each year. (This fragment could also be written as a question or in another way.)

12   The Five Ws and an H

Right from the start, every reporter learns the importance of six questions. Called the five Ws and an H, they form the basis of an interview. They are questions the reporter keeps in mind when writing the lead, or opening paragraph, of a news story. After a while, they become second nature.

These are the questions all reporters learn to ask:

Who

What

When

Where

Why

How

Just as in news writing, the five Ws and an H answer essential questions in grammar.

- Who or what is the sentence about? . . . finds the subject.

- What did or does the subject do? . . . finds the verb.

- Who or what? . . . identifies all nouns and pronouns, including the subject.

- What kind of or what number of? . . . is answered by an adjective.

- Adverbs answer the other questions: When? Where? Why? How?

USING THE FIVE Ws AND AN H

Reading is not just passing your eyes over words and, like a camera, recording a mass of facts and information. The good reader is busy asking questions: Who or what? Is doing what? Where? When? How? Why?

These questions not only help the reader pick out words and give them grammatical labels; the questions also help find meaning.

When something is hard to understand, the good reader can turn to grammar. By identifying key words and seeing what questions they answer, someone who knows how grammar works can more easily arrive at an understanding of what even the most difficult-seeming sentences mean.

An understanding of grammar can help clarify the connection of ideas in all kinds of writing, from newspaper stories to poetry, from technical writing to fiction.

To discover how grammar can help, read these lead paragraphs from a newspaper story.

CROWDED U.S. AIRPORTS THREATENED BY GRIDLOCK

The nation's major airports, a vast, varied, and aging collection of former farm fields and swamps, are rapidly approaching gridlock. The overworked facilities funnel more than 450 million passengers into high-flying jets traveling more than one-half billion miles annually.

According to experts, paralysis looms within five years and threatens the $57 billion-a-year airline industry, the nation's international competitiveness, countless local economies, and some fundamental assumptions about the American way of life.

What is the S-V-C in the first sentence?

(S-V-C)   airports/are approaching/gridlock

What is the purpose of the words between *a vast* and *swamps*? *Collection* is the first noun you find in this phrase. An appositive, the entire phrase is used to further identify airports.

What kind of collection? <u>of fields and swamps</u>

Grammar can help clear up the picture. The nation's airports are a vast, varied, and aging collection. They are built on former farm fields and swamps. They are fast approaching gridlock.

The S-V-C of the second sentence is:

(S-V-C)   Facilities/funnel/passengers

Where do they "funnel passengers"? <u>into jets</u>

What kind of jets? <u>high-flying jets</u>
<u>jets that travel more than one-half billion miles</u>

When do they travel this distance? <u>annually</u>

How and why are they overworked? It should be easy to draw the right conclusion:

<u>They are old, yet they carry over 450 million passengers annually.</u>

The third sentence says that "paralysis looms. . . and threatens." Threatens what? The verb *threatens* has four nouns as complements. These four nouns explain what is threatened: the industry, U.S. competitiveness, local economics, and some assumptions. Using grammar to find the complements brings out these key points. To go further into the details, check the adjectives that modify each noun. Some sentences are packed with meaning. Grammar can help you strip them down to their essentials.

PUTTING YOUR KNOWLEDGE OF GRAMMAR TO WORK

Often the first, most important step in reading is to orient yourself by finding the S-V-C of problem sentences. This lets you know the underlying idea upon which the entire sentence is based.

The Five Ws and an H provide the answers that let you go on to ask further questions such as

What is the author's purpose?

Why did he or she say that?

How does it all fit together?

Knowing the right questions is often just as important as knowing the answers. It gives you a place to start and somewhere to go.

At this point in grammar, there is still much to learn. In reading, concentrate on determining meaningful answers to the five Ws and an H. It's not necessary, or even helpful, to attempt to pinpoint the exact grammatical usage of every word or phrase.

SELF-TEST

What are the "secrets" of a poem? Believe it or not, grammar often helps supply the answer, and it helps you get to the heart of poetry, too.

Part of the beauty of poetry comes from the way the poet puts words together, using the order and balance of grammar to bring out the poem's meaning.

You don't have to know the definition of every word to understand what you read, nor should you take time to look up every word you don't know in the dictionary. Work from what you do know, and with the help of grammar, you can add to your vocabulary in the act of reading.

Read the following poem by Elinor Wylie. When you've finished the poem and the questions following it, you'll know why the poem itself isn't what you might expect from its title.

Sea Lullaby
The old moon is tarnished
With smoke of the flood,
The dead leaves are varnished
With color like blood.

A treacherous smiler
With teeth white as milk,
A savage beguiler
In sheathings of silk,

The sea creeps to pillage,
She leaps on her prey;
A child of the village
Was murdered today.

She came up to meet him
In a smooth golden cloak.
She choked him and beat him
To death, for a joke.

Her bright locks were tangled,
She shouted for joy,
With one hand she strangled
A strong little boy.

Now in silence she lingers
Beside him all night
To wash her long fingers
In silvery light.

Using the Five Ws and an H, along with grammar as your aid, decide your answers to the following questions.

1. The first two sets of subject/verb are a. [The] moon/is tarnished and b. [The] leaves/are varnished. What prepositional phrases answer *how* for each?
   a. _____
   b. _____

2. The next subject/verb doesn't come until the third stanza: [The] sea/ creeps. What nouns in the second stanza are used in apposition to *sea?*

   _____

3. Considering the poem's title, what surprising adjectives describe these nouns and also the sea? _____

4. See how the S-Vs tell the story:

   She/leaps
   [A] child/was murdered
   She/choked/him
   [and] beat/him
   [Her] locks/were tangled
   She/shouted
   she/strangled

   Working from the subjects, verbs, and complements, what answers do you find to the Five Ws and an H about each S-V-C? _____

   _____

   _____

   _____

5. The end of the poem states she/lingers. Where? _____
   When? _____ Why? _____

6. What attitude does the poem create toward the boy? Through what words? _____

   _____

7. The poem personifies the sea, speaking of it as if it were a woman and calling it "she." What attitude does the poem create toward this "woman," the sea? _____

   _____

8. What words describe its beauty? _____

   _____

   _____

9. What words indicate that the sea kills, not out of hate or anger but because it is part of the sea's nature? _____

   _____

10. In what ways can the sea's behavior fit the idea of its "lullabying" the child, even though in a horrible way? _____

    _____

    _____

ANSWERS

1. a. with smoke of the flood; b. with color like blood 2. smiler; beguiler 3. savage and treacherous 4. Leaps how? on her prey; What child? of the village; When? today; Choked

and beat how? to death; Why? for a joke; Shouted why? for joy 5. Where? beside him; When? now, all night; Why? to wash . . . in silvery light 6. The poem creates a sympathetic attitude. The boy was strong and little; he was killed for no good reason. 7. The sea was beautiful, untrustworthy, and cruel. The attitude is one of horror, but also awe for the sea's beauty and power. 8. white as milk, sheathings of silk, smooth golden cloak, bright locks 9. for a joke, shouted for joy, lingers beside him 10. "In silence she lingers" fits the idea of the sea's lullabying the dead child while her waves rock him.

13 The Amazing Word *Be* and Its Many Faces

What do the words *is, was, am,* and *are* have in common? They are all forms of exactly the same verb, which goes by the family name of *be*. *Be* is the most irregular of all the irregular verbs. The three principal parts of *be*—*am, is, are* in the present tense—are *be, was, been.* Other verbs, such as *go* (*go, went, gone*) and *eat* (*eat, ate, eaten*), also have parts that differ greatly from their root word or **infinitive.** Yet their family resemblances are closer than those of *be*.

A DEFECTIVE VERB

How can such different-looking words actually be the same word? The dictionary calls *be* a defective verb because it gets its three principal parts from three unrelated stems or sources. Defective or not, *be* is in constant use and has many different purposes. It works, and no one has ever gotten around to fixing it so it works more smoothly.

Here are the grammatically accepted forms of be in its primary and perfect tenses.

Present Tense

I <u>am</u>   We <u>are</u>

You <u>are</u>   You <u>are</u>

He/she/it <u>is</u>   They <u>are</u>

Past Tense

I <u>was</u>   We <u>were</u>

You <u>were</u>   You <u>were</u>

He/she/it <u>was</u>   They <u>were</u>

Future Tense

I <u>will be</u>	We <u>will be</u>
You <u>will be</u>	You <u>will be</u>
He/she/it <u>will be</u>	They <u>will be</u>

Present Perfect Tense

I <u>have been</u>	We <u>have been</u>
You <u>have been</u>	You <u>have been</u>
He/she/it <u>has been</u>	They <u>have been</u>

Past Perfect Tense

I <u>had been</u>	We <u>had been</u>
You <u>had been</u>	You <u>had been</u>
He/she/it <u>had been</u>	They <u>had been</u>

Future Perfect Tense

I <u>will have been</u>	We <u>will have been</u>
You <u>will have been</u>	You <u>will have been</u>
He/she/it <u>will have been</u>	They <u>will have been</u>

USES OF *BE*

Be is often used as a linking verb, but it's much more than that. The dictionary definition of *be* is "to live, to happen, to remain or continue, or to belong to." In some sentences, it seems to mean "to cost, to look, or to signify."

To understand how *be* works, consider its uses one by one.

Be *as a Linking Verb*

- Stephanie <u>is</u> an actress.
  (S-V-C) Stephanie/is/[an] actress

- Puppies <u>are</u> playful.
  (S-V-C) Puppies/are/playful

- Marty <u>will be</u> ready soon.
  (S-V-C) Marty/will be/ready

- <u>Is</u> Brad your only brother?
  (S-V-C) Brad/is/brother

Actress and *brother*, which rename or identify the subject, are called **predicate nouns.** *Playful* and *ready*, which describe the subject, are **predicate adjectives.** All four words are **subjective complements** because they relate back to the subject.

Other verbs work as linking verbs in the same way (for example, *seem* and *feel*), but none is put to work so often as *be*.

TIP

Of course, *be* can take all the other helpers to form verb phrases; *can be, will be, must be, would have been, should have been, might have been,* and so on.

In the following sentences, identify the S-V-C. Then tell whether each complement is a predicate noun or predicate adjective. Be sure to include helping verbs and be alert for compound parts.

1. My friend Alain is a wonderful cook.

2. Meals at Alain's are almost always delicious and sometimes fattening.

3. Alain's specialties have usually been French dishes.

4. Alain's menus can never be simple.

5. Only one was a spectacular flop.

6. His main course should have been awesome.

7. Instead, it was nearly inedible.

8. Without dessert, the dinner would have been a total disaster.

S-V-C	Type of Complement
1. _____	_____
2. _____	_____
3. _____	_____
4. _____	_____
5. _____	_____
6. _____	_____

S-V-C	Type of Complement
7. _____	_____
8. _____	_____

Answers: 1. (S-V-C) friend/is/cook; pred. noun 2. (S-V-C) Meals/are/delicious, fattening; pred. adj. 3. (S-V-C) specialties/have been/dishes; pred. noun 4. (S-V-C) menus/can be/simple; pred. adj. 5. (S-V-C) one/was/flop; pred. noun 6. (S-V-C) course/should have been/awesome; pred. adj. 7. (S-V-C) it/was/inedible; pred. adj. 8. (S-V-C) dinner/would have been/disaster; pred. noun

Be *as an Intransitive Verb*

- Your wallet <u>is</u> on the chest of drawers.

- Jake <u>is</u> in a hurry.

- Summer <u>will be</u> here soon.

- The performance <u>is</u> at 8 o'clock.

Notice that there is no answer if you use the verb and ask "What?" after it. Therefore, none of these sentences has a complement. All of the elements after the verb in the examples work as adverbs. In all four sentences, *be* works as an **intransitive verb**—that is, one that has no complement.

HOW THE WORD *THERE* WORKS WITH *BE*

- Where is it? It is there.

Both of these sentences have the same S-V: it/is. Both *where* and *there* are adverbs.
   Now consider these sentences.

- There <u>is</u> no doubt about the outcome.
   (S-V) doubt/is

- There <u>is</u> a prediction of snow for tomorrow.
   (S-V) prediction/is

In neither sentence does *there* answer the question "Where?" Yet, both sentences sound incomplete when the word *there* is omitted:

- No doubt about the outcome <u>is</u>.

- A prediction of snow for tomorrow <u>is</u>.

In both sentences, *be* is an intransitive verb that expresses the state of being. *There* is simply an introductory word. It fills out the sentence and acts as a balance on one side of the verb *be* for true subject on the other. In such sentences, *there* is not an adverb. It's called an **expletive;** its job is to let the subject come later. Don't be fooled into calling it the subject.

Note: *It* can also be used as an expletive.

Example: <u>It</u> is not likely that she'll come.

In the following sentences, identify the S-V-C or S-V to see whether *be* is used as a linking or intransitive verb. If *be* has a complement, decide whether it's a predicate noun or a predicate adjective.

1.   Ernie is the team's leading scorer.

2.   Paula has always been very good at tennis.

3.   Someday Matt will be either in an executive suite or in prison.

4.   Beryl, you can be so difficult at times.

5.   There might not be enough for everyone at the party.

6.   Julie would have been my choice for the job.

7.   Be careful of that slippery spot on the sidewalk.

	S-V-C	Type of Verb	Type of Complement, If Any
1.	_____	_____	_____
2.	_____	_____	_____
3.	_____	_____	_____
4.	_____	_____	_____
5.	_____	_____	_____

S-V-C	Type of Verb	Type of Complement, If Any
6. _____	_____	_____
7. _____	_____	_____

Answers: 1. (S-V-C) Ernie/is/scorer; linking; pred. noun 2. (S-V-C) Paula/has been/good; linking; pred. adj 3. (S-V) Matt/will be; intrans. 4. (S-V-C) you/can be/difficult; linking; pred. adj 5. (S-V) enough/might be; intrans. 6. (S-V-C) Julie/would have been/choice; linking; pred. noun 7. (S-V-C) you/be/careful; linking; pred. adj.

PROGRESSIVE VERB PHRASES

What is the difference in meaning between each of the following pairs?

Flip <u>talks</u>	Flip <u>is talking</u>
Bea <u>swims</u>	Bea <u>is swimming</u>
Cathy <u>laughs</u>	Cathy <u>is laughing</u>
you <u>practice</u>	you <u>are practicing</u>
I <u>drive</u>	I <u>am driving</u>
they <u>go</u>	they <u>are going</u>

Although both deal with the present, those in the second column tell of an act in progress. The first column, actually in the present tense, tells of a habitual act and means, for example, that Flip can and does talk but may not be talking at the moment. "Flip is talking" means it's happening now.

Be + the *-ing* form of the verb = the **progressive**

The *-ing* form of the verb is called the **present participle.**

Be works as a helper to determine the time of the action in progress.

progressive present

I am working; he/she/it is working; we/you/they are working

progressive past

I/he/she/it was working; we/you/they were working

progressive future

will be working (for all personal pronouns)

progressive present perfect

I/we/you/they have been working; he/she/it has been working

progressive past perfect

had been working (for all personal pronouns)

progressive future perfect

will have been working (for all personal pronouns)

FORMING THE PRESENT PARTICIPLE

There's no trick to forming the present participle. Just add *-ing* to the base of the verb. Even *be* is regular; it becomes *being*.

Some verbs, such as *get, sit,* and *bat,* double their final consonant to keep the short sound of a vowel: *getting, sitting, batting.* Others drop an *e* before *-ing.* Examples are *become, rate,* and *bite.* Their present participles are *becoming, rating,* and *biting.* Just compare *matting* with *mating* to see why such changes are necessary.

When in doubt, check the dictionary. As with other verb forms, if the *-ing* form isn't listed, you may assume it neither doubles a letter nor drops an *e.*

When a verb is progressive, there are always two or more words in its verb string. Last comes the present participle that tells what the subject does or is doing. As with any verb, the progressive may or may not have a complement. It can be transitive, intransitive, or linking.

- Chet has been working at the Blanchard Company for three years.
    (S-V) Chet/has been working
        Intransitive; has no object

- Joyce is buying a new car, a Jeep Explorer.
    (S-V-C) Joyce/is buying/[a] car
        Transitive; direct object, car

- The defense witness was acting very hesitant about all of his answers.
    (S-V-C) [The] witness/was acting/hesitant
        Linking; complement, hesitant (a predicate adjective)

Identify the S-V-C or S-V of each of the following sentences. Determine whether the verbs are intransitive, transitive, or linking. If there is a complement, decide whether it is a direct object, predicate adjective, or predicate noun.

1. We are counting on you for help.

2. Nora and Ted have been saving their money for a new house.

3. For a change, the baby was being an absolute angel.

4. The company will be using a new phone system in the future.

5. You are really promising a great deal.

6. Without our knowledge, a chipmunk had been nibbling blossoms off the plants.

7. In a few minutes, we will have been waiting for Jerry for exactly two hours.

8. Why are you leaving the party so early?

	S-V-C or S-V	Type of Verb	Type of Complement, If Any
1.	_____	_____	_____
2.	_____	_____	_____
3.	_____	_____	_____
4.	_____	_____	_____
5.	_____	_____	_____
6.	_____	_____	_____
7.	_____	_____	_____
8.	_____	_____	_____

Answers: 1. We/are counting; intrans. 2. Nora [and] Ted/have been saving/money; trans.; dir. obj. 3. baby/was being/angel; linking; pred. noun 4. company/will be using/system; trans.; dir. obj. 5. You/are promising/deal; trans.; dir. obj. 6. chipmunk/ had been nibbling/blossoms; trans.; dir. obj. 7. we/will have been waiting; intrans. 8. you/are leaving/party; trans.; dir. obj.

THE VOICE OF VERBS: ACTIVE OR PASSIVE

Verbs do more than express meaning. You've seen how verbs express time or tense. They also have a quality called **voice.** Verbs have two voices, **active** and **passive.** Voice is easiest to understand when you see it in action.

- The committee chose Kyle as Salesman of the Year.
  (S-V-C) [The] committee/chose/Kyle

- Kyle was chosen as Salesman of the Year by the committee.
  (S-V) Kyle/was chosen

The first example is active: the Subject-Verb is acting upon the object, Kyle. The second example is passive. The former object, Kyle, is now the subject and passively takes the action of the verb. The subject of the first sentence becomes an object of the preposition in the second.

Of course, only a verb that can take an object—that is, a transitive verb—works in the passive voice.

Why does English need a passive voice? Some might answer, "It doesn't." Some writers try hard to avoid using the passive voice because they want their words to sound active. Notice the disadvantages of the passive voice in the examples below.

- The writer quoted an incorrect percentage in the article.

- An incorrect percentage was quoted in the article by the writer.

- An incorrect percentage was quoted in the article.

The second sentence uses eleven words to say exactly the same thing that the first says in nine. The third example uses only eight words, but omits information that may be important.

In addition, the passive voice doesn't carry the idea forward as forcefully as the active voice does.

There are, however, advantages to the passive voice. The first question to ask about a sentence is, "Who or what is it about?" In the second example, the answer is *percentage.* In the first, active voice makes it *writer.*

Word order is important in English, and the passive voice gives a prominent position to a word that would come after the verb in the active voice. Passive voice turns the receiver of an action, the object, into the subject.

In this case, *writer* isn't very important. (All articles have writers.) So the third example is probably the best of the three. But if you wish to emphasize a particular writer as being at fault, the active voice is preferable.

- (weak) The wrong percentage was quoted by Froyden in his article.

- (better) Froyden quoted the wrong percentage in his article.

FORMING THE PASSIVE VOICE

The passive voice works best when the agent, or former subject, is not essential to the sentence. In any case, avoid its overuse.

passive voice = the helping verb *be* + the past participle of the verb

1. Use *be* in the same tense in which the basic verb would be in the active voice.

2. The past participle is the third principal part of the verb.

Examples
Note the changes in the Subject-Verb in the following.

- (active) Senator Bacon <u>gave</u> the keynote address at the convention.
  (passive) The keynote address at the convention <u>was given</u> by Senator Bacon.

- (active) We have not <u>revealed</u> our plans to anyone.
  (passive) Our plans <u>have</u> not <u>been revealed</u> to anyone [by us].

- (active) Heavy air traffic <u>causes</u> long delays at the nation's major airports.
  (passive) Long delays at the nation's major airports <u>are caused</u> by heavy air traffic.

Identify the S-V-C or S-V of each sentence, and decide whether the verb is in the active or passive voice. Rewrite each sentence using the opposite voice. Notice that the agent of the action is often missing from the passive voice. When this occurs, supply a subject for the active voice.

1. The lawyer questioned Sylvia about her whereabouts on the night of May 17.

   S-V-C or S-V _____ Active or Passive _____

   Revision _____

   _____

2. Many of the regular shows were not televised Monday because of the President's speech.

S-V-C or S-V _____ Active or Passive _____

Revision _____

_____

3. People around the world will have heard the news at almost the same instant.

S-V-C or S-V _____ Active or Passive _____

Revision _____

_____

4. The latest pictures of Nelson's grandson are shown to everyone.

S-V-C or S-V _____ Active or Passive _____

Revision _____

_____

5. The Oscar for best picture will be given last.

S-V-C or S-V _____ Active or Passive _____

Revision _____

_____

6. Most of the chocolate cake was eaten by my little brother.

S-V-C or S-V _____ Active or Passive _____

Revision _____

_____

7. I have spoken my last word on the subject.

S-V-C or S-V _____ Active or Passive _____

Revision _____

_____

Answers: 1. (S-V-C) [The] lawyer/questioned/Sylvia; active; Sylvia was questioned by the lawyer about her whereabouts on the night of May 17. 2. (S-V) Many/

were [not] televised; passive; The networks did not televise many of the regular shows Monday because of the President's speech. 3. (S-V-C) People/will have heard/news; active; The news will have been heard by people around the world at almost the same instant. 4. (S-V) Pictures/are shown; passive; Nelson shows the latest pictures of his grandson to everyone. 5. (S-V) [The] Oscar/will be given; passive; The Motion Picture Academy will give the Oscar for best picture last. 6. (S-V) Most/was eaten; passive; My little brother ate most of the chocolate cake. 7. (S-V-C) I/have spoken/word; active; My last word on the subject has been spoken.

SELF-TEST

Underline the complete verb. Then indicate whether *be* is used as a linking verb, intransitive, progressive tense auxiliary verb, or passive voice auxiliary.

1. Are you more enthusiastic about dinosaurs or UFOs? _____

2. There has been great interest in dinosaurs lately. _____

3. Dinosaurs have been proved to exist in ancient times. _____

4. According to some people, there may have been visitors to Earth from outer space, as well. _____

5. Believers in UFOs are still looking for evidence to convince nonbelievers. _____

6. Both dinosaurs and UFOs have been subjects of many books and films. _____

7. Exhibits of dinosaurs can be found in many museums. _____

8. The best science fiction is based on possibilities, not on pure fantasy.
   _____

9. The lure of the unknown is continuing to fire people's imaginations.
   _____

ANSWERS

1. are; linking 2. has been; intransitive 3. have been proved; passive 4. may have been; intransitive 5. are looking; progressive 6. have been; linking 7. can be found; passive 8. is based; passive 9. is continuing; progressive

14 More about Pronouns and Nouns

Personal pronouns are needed to take the place of nouns, but the fact that each has several forms can cause confusion.

Some people choose and use the wrong pronouns for a number of reasons. They may not understand how pronouns work. They may have a habit of using pronouns incorrectly and find it hard to break, even though they know better. They may even think the correct forms sound too stuffy and artificial. Yet even in conversation, certain mistakes in pronouns act just like a spot of salsa on a new outfit. They spoil the effect completely.

CASE

Case is the term given to the form taken by a word, such as a pronoun, to express and clarify its relationship to other words in a sentence.

The Nominative Case

Use the **nominative** case for:

- a pronoun used as subject of a sentence or clause telling who or what it's about

    Example: <u>She</u> is the winner.

- a predicate nominative that follows a linking verb and renames the subject

    Example: It is <u>I</u> who called.

The Objective Case

Use the **objective** case for:

- a pronoun used as a direct object of a verb

    Example: The judges unanimously selected <u>her</u>.

- the object of a preposition.

    Example: It was a great honor for <u>her</u>.

Most other uses of pronouns in the objective case will fall naturally into place if you understand these.

The following table shows how first and third person pronouns change according to use. *You* and *it* don't change in these two cases.

		Nominative case	Objective case
Singular	1st Person	I	me
	2nd Person	you	you
	3rd Person	he, she, it	him, her, it
Plural	1st Person	we	us
	2nd Person	you	you
	3rd Person	they	them

In English, nouns don't have different forms for the nominative and objective cases but most personal pronouns do. That's why it's so important to understand the case uses, shared by nouns and pronouns, to know the right pronouns to choose.

Note how case use determines which pronouns are chosen to replace the nouns in each example.

- <u>Helen</u> hates <u>Herbert</u>. (Helen is the subject; Herbert, the direct object.)
  <u>She</u> hates <u>him</u>.

- We bought a wedding present for <u>Carol</u> and <u>Ken</u>.
  (Both Carol and Ken are objects of the preposition.)
  We bought a wedding present for <u>them</u>.

- My <u>friends and I</u> disagree about the use of nuclear power.
  (Friends and I are the compound subject.)
  <u>We</u> disagree about it.

- The caller was <u>Slade</u>.
  (Slade is a predicate nominative.)
  The caller was <u>he</u>.

That last sentence may sound strange and artificial, but using the nominative case of the pronoun as a predicate nominative is the grammatically correct choice, according to the way the pronoun is working. Should you sound stuffy and be right, or follow informal usage and be wrong? Modern speakers who know the rules of grammar sometimes rephrase a sentence to avoid having to make such a decision. In this case, you could say, "He was the caller."

Training yourself to choose and use pronouns correctly is a key factor in grammar. The ability to recognize and use the right pronoun is taken as the mark of someone who cares about language and who values precision in speaking and writing.

For each of the following sentences, first decide whether a word in the blank space would serve as a subject, direct object, object of a preposition, or predicate nominative. Then fill in the blank with any personal pronoun (except *you* or *it*) that makes sense and is in the right case.

1. In my opinion, _____ is someone who takes too many chances.

2. Debbie decided not to wait for Paco and _____ any longer.

3. At the beginning of the story, I never suspected that the murderer would be _____ .

4. Mr. and Mrs. Cleveland want you to tell _____ about your trip.

5. Both you and _____ are in the running for the award.

6. This is a secret I want kept strictly between _____ two.

7. The benefactor hoped no one would suspect the donor was _____ .

8. Barbie and Bobby's mother often dresses _____ both in the same color to show _____ are twins.

Answers: 1. she or he 2. me, him, her, them, or us 3. he or she 4. me, him, her, them, or us 5. I, he, she, they 6. us 7. he or she 8. them, they

Warning: Compound Pronouns at Work

The correct choice of pronouns is hardest to figure out when they're compound. Almost no one would think it sounded right to ask, "Is this for I?" Yet, for some reason, when two pronouns or a noun and a pronoun are joined, making the correct choice gets confusing.

It's essential to remember that the coordinating conjunctions (*and, but, or,* etc.) join two equal parts. When it comes to pronouns, that means you should always pair two matching pronouns of the same case: *he and she; him and her; we and they; us and them.* When a noun is paired with a pronoun, as in the sentence "Mary and (I, me) are good friends," be sure to check their use in the sentence. In this case, they are compound subjects; the right choice is "Mary and I."

In each of the following sentences, first identify the S-V-C. Then list each pronoun, along with its use in the sentence.

1. Between you and me, we will make a success of the project.

2. Both Rob and I thank you for coming.

3. It was not a friendly argument but a matter of them against us.

4. The last to leave the party were Molly and I.

5. My sister and I should be able to help you.

6. The practical joke did not strike Rick and me as particularly funny.

S-V-C	Pronouns, Case Uses
1. _____	_____
2. _____	_____
3. _____	_____
4. _____	_____
5. _____	_____
6. _____	_____

Answers: 1. (S-V-C) we/will make/success; you, me/obj. of prep.; we/subj. 2. (S-V-C) Rob [and] I/thank/you; I/subj.; you/dir. obj. 3. (S-V-C) It/was/argument [but] matter; It/subj.; them/obj. prep.; us/obj. prep. 4. (S-V-C) last/were/Molly [and] I; I/pred. noun 5. (S-V-C) sister [and] I/should be able; I/sub.; you/dir. obj. 6. (S-V-C) joke/did strike/ Rick [and] me; me/dir. obj.

MORE ABOUT THE OBJECTIVE CASE

So far, you have seen two kinds of objects: direct object and object of a preposition. Here are three more ways verbs make objects of nouns and pronouns.

Indirect Object

- Nan brought her hosts a bottle of wine.

Brought whom or what? Both *hosts* and *bottle* answer the question.

In this example, *bottle* is the **direct object**; *hosts* is an **indirect object**, which names to or for whom or what an action is being done. (Notice that the sentence works without its indirect object, *hosts*, but doesn't without the direct object, *bottle*.)

Here are two ways to check and make sure you've found an indirect object.

1. Indirect objects come before a direct object.

2. You can turn the indirect object into an object of a preposition, using *to* or *for*. See how this works with the example given:

- Nan brought a bottle of wine for her hosts.

Only certain verbs can take indirect objects. They include *give, take, bring, offer,* and *tell*.

In each of the following sentences, change the indirect object into a prepositional phrase.

1. Clark told the police officer the truth.

_____

2. The boss has offered Andrea a promotion.

_____

3. Give me your attention.

_____

4. It should only take me a minute to finish this puzzle.

_____

Answers: 1. Clark told the truth to the police officer. 2. The boss offered a promotion to Andrea. 3. Give your attention to me. 4. It should only take a minute for me to finish this puzzle.

Objective Complement

- The Liars Club elected Sally president.

Elected whom or what? <u>Sally</u> Elected her what? <u>president</u>

In this sentence, the direct object, *Sally,* comes first and its complement, *president,* follows. In this type of sentence, *president* is called an **objective complement,** because it completes the meaning of the object.

Here are three points to remember about objective complements:

1. The objective complement renames the object, just as a subjective complement renames or modifies the subject.

   • The team has chosen Blaine captain.

   • Some people would label Theo a loner.

2. Objective complements can be adjectives, as well as nouns or pronouns in the objective case.

   • Are you calling me lazy?

   • She considers him charming.

3. Only certain verbs can have objective complements. They include *call, name, choose, consider,* and *label.*

If you are not sure whether a word is an objective complement, check by putting *as* or *to be* before it and after the direct object. The resulting version ought to make sense.

• The team has chosen Blaine as captain.

Retained Object

• Andrea has been offered a promotion by her boss.

• Art Tatum is considered a piano genius by jazz fans.

• He would be labeled a loner by some people.

Do you recognize these sentences? They are recast versions of examples for indirect objects and objective complements. In each, the verb is now in the passive voice and one of the objects has become a subject. Here are the (S-Vs) of those sentences.

• Andrea/has been offered

• Art Tatum/is considered

• He/would be labeled

Since verbs in passive voice cannot have objects, the "leftovers" (*promotion, genius,* and *loner*) are called **retained objects**. This means that their sense as an object is kept, even though the verb isn't active. Because they are nouns, they answer the question "what?", but they are not direct objects because the Subject-Verb is not acting upon them. It was the boss who offered Andrea the promotion; she is not involved in the action.

This is another example of the importance of word order to English. If a sentence in the passive voice is difficult to understand, it is often helpful to change the word order and consider the sentence in the active voice, thereby clarifying its meaning. Only sentences that would have indirect objects or objective complements in the active voice can have retained objects.

- Active Voice: Clark told the police officer the truth.
  indirect object = the police officer

- Passive Voice: The police officer was told the truth by Clark.
  retained object = the truth

Identify the use of the underlined nouns and pronouns in the following sentences. They may be direct object, indirect object, object of preposition, retained object, or objective complement.

1. Please give <u>me</u> a <u>summary</u> of your <u>findings</u>.

_____

2. The boss considers <u>Annetta</u> a natural <u>leader</u>.

_____

3. She was recently named <u>manager</u> of her <u>division</u>.

_____

4. Annetta told <u>me</u> and the <u>rest</u> of the staff the good <u>news</u> this morning.

_____

5. She naturally was given a healthy <u>raise</u> along with the <u>promotion</u>.

_____

Answers: 1. me/ind. obj.; summary/dir. obj.; findings/obj. prep. 2. Annetta/dir. obj.; leader/obj. comp. 3. manager/ret. obj.; division/obj. prep. 4. me, rest/ind. obj.; staff/obj. prep.; news/dir. obj. 5. raise/ret. obj.; promotion/obj. prep.

WORD ORDER MAKES ENGLISH WORK

What words are nouns? Verbs? Adjectives? Without a sentence, it's nearly impossible to say for sure. For instance, is *light* a noun? It all depends, as you can see in the following sentences.

- The <u>light</u> was dazzling. (noun)

- Fireworks <u>light</u> up the sky. (verb)

- Bring a <u>light</u> jacket. (adjective)

- The child skipped <u>lightly</u>. (slightly changed, now an adverb)

In some languages it's much easier to identify a part of speech by word endings or inflections, but in English you need to see a word at work before you can be sure.

To discover the possible uses of a specific word, look it up in a good dictionary.

POSSESSIVES

How do the underlined words work in the following sentences? What questions do they answer?

- That is <u>Mario's</u> jacket.

- The <u>boys'</u> bedroom is a mess.

- What is <u>Mr. Aiken's</u> opinion?

All three seem to answer the question "What one or whose?" What jacket, bedroom, or opinion? Therefore, they do the work of an adjective.

Some grammarians, basing their description of English on the grammatical systems of ancient Latin and Greek, would say that these examples belong to a third case of nouns, the possessive case. Actually, many words well known as nouns in English often show up as adjectives, even without a change of ending.

- The <u>storm</u> clouds hung overhead and darkened the sky.

- Our brains are our <u>message</u> centers.

It's easier, in fact, to see possessives as pronoun forms acting as adjectives. Their purpose is to indicate ownership or belonging.

Possessive Forms

In the possessive singular, nouns take an apostrophe followed by an *s*:

> author's imagination
>
> girl's dream
>
> horse's speed
>
> Bess's luck
>
> engineer's opinion

In the plural, most nouns just add an apostrophe after their regular sign of the plural:

> farmers' crops
>
> Giants' victory
>
> cats' personalities,
>
> Indians' culture
>
> jokers' pranks

To plurals that don't end in *s,* an apostrophe plus *s* (*'s*) is added

> children's mittens
>
> women's viewpoints
>
> sheep's wool, geese's formation
>
> deer's coloring

When in doubt, check the dictionary; it will help with irregular forms for plurals.

Personal pronouns have two forms to use as possessives. The first is for use as a possessive adjective:

	Singular	Plural
1st Person	my	our
2nd Person	your	your
3rd Person	his, her, its	their

The second is for use in place of a noun:

	Singular	Plural
1st Person	mine	ours
2nd Person	yours	yours
3rd Person	his, hers, its	theirs

Note that *his* and *its* are both possessive adjectives and pronouns.

Here are some possessive forms in action. In the blank space after each sentence, label each of the underlined words according to its use: as a pronoun or an adjective.

1. Where are your crayons? _____

2. Those are mine; this box is his. _____ _____

3. Hers has more colors than yours or mine.

_____ _____ _____

4. Let's share ours. Buddy and Bonnie forgot theirs. _____ _____

Answers: 1. adjective 2. both pronouns 3. all pronouns 4. both pronouns

Like the possessive pronouns and adjectives, possessive nouns also can serve as modifiers or stand alone:

• Sarah's hair is blond. Lou's is a bit darker.

Using Apostrophes Correctly

With personal pronouns, apostrophes replace missing letters in contractions. For example:

I'm = I am you're = you are it's = it is, it has
I've = I have he'd = he had, he would we'll = we will

Be sure it would make sense to substitute *it is* or *it has* before you write *it's*.

- <u>It's</u> a tune I can't forget.
  <u>It is</u> a tune I can't forget.

In the sentence above, the apostrophe is correctly used.

- I like that song, but I can never remember <u>its</u> name.

In this case, *its* is correct. You don't mean "it is name."
  Other frequently confused pairs are *your* and *you're* and *their* and *they're*. None of the possessive pronoun forms should be used with an apostrophe. Check the following correct examples:

- The dog's leash is hanging behind the door.
  Its leash is hanging behind the door.

- Is this Vicki's briefcase?
  Is this her briefcase?
  Is this hers?

Remember that it's important to use an apostrophe in contractions. (It's the right way to make short work of *it is*.) But a pronoun never uses an apostrophe to form its possessive. (Its formation of the possessive is different from a noun's.)

SELF-TEST

1. After determining the needed case, write your choice of the words in parentheses in the blank space.

   a. With Rob and _____ (she, her) as candidates, it will be a difficult choice.

   b. Was a postcard from Vic or _____ (they, them) in today's mail?

   c. Along with Sue and _____ (he, him,) Nat has asked Trish and _____ (I, me) to serve on the welcoming committee.

   d. Without a doubt, both _____ (we, us) and _____ (they, them) were interested in Larry's suggestion.

   e. Neither Rosa nor _____ (he, him) would be my choice for the position.

f. Both Hugh and _____ (I, me) have brought enough potato salad for a thousand hungry ants.

g. According to Mr. Walsh, the mechanic offered a guarantee on the brake job to his wife and _____ (he, him).

h. In sports and world affairs, people are too often divided into _____ (we, us) and _____ (they, them).

i. Gloria, were you and _____ (he, him) kidding when you asked if Mark or _____ (I, me) wanted to ride along?

ANSWERS

a. her b. them c. him; me d. we; they e. he f. I g. him h. us; them i. he; I

2. In the blank spaces, write the correct form of the word in parentheses. If it is a noun, choose between whether it should end in 's or s'.

a. The _____ basketball game was delayed because of a power outage. (men)

b. There is very little difference between _____ plan and _____ . (I; you.)

c. The _____ wishes were granted. (child)

d. Both her maternal and paternal _____ homes are in Florida. (grandparents)

e. One of the _____ biggest attractions is Disney World. (state)

f. Her _____ parents live in Orlando. (father)

g. Of the two, _____ is her favorite home to visit. (their)

ANSWERS

a. men's b. my; yours c. child's d. grandparents' e. state's f. father's g. theirs

3. Note and correct any errors in the use of pronouns in the following sentences. Add apostrophes where needed in contractions.

a. Its not my idea. _____

b. Im not certain of it's price. _____

c. Youre right in your estimate of the distance. _____

d. Hers' is the only gift he's bought so far. _____

e. Theirs nothing here but their footprints. _____

ANSWERS

a. It's b. I'm; its c. You're d. Hers e. There's

15　Introducing the Verbals

A **verbal** is a verb form serving not as part of the S-V or S-V-C of a clause but as another part of speech. Verbals are easier to understand when you see them in action.

Here's how the dictionary lists the principal parts of the irregular verb *grow*, along with their pronunciation:

> grow [grō] v.i. [GREW [groo], GROWN [grōn], GROWING]—Also, v.t.

Unlike the irregular verbs, the principal parts of regular verbs such as talk [talked, talked, talking] are not shown in the dictionary.

PARTICIPLES AT WORK

It's clearer to see how the principal parts work with an irregular verb such as *grow*. The third principal part of the verb is called the **past participle**. It always needs a helper to act as the main verb in a sentence or clause. It's used in the perfect tenses and in passive voice. Here are examples of *grown*, the past participle of *grow*, at work in sentences.

- Danny <u>has grown</u>.
- Soybeans <u>are grown</u> by many Midwestern farmers.

The *-ing* form of the verb, or its **present participle**, works with *be* in all the progressive verb phrases. [For a review, see Chapter 13.)

- We <u>are growing</u>.
- We <u>will be growing</u>.
- We <u>had been growing</u>.

You can think of the term *participle* as showing that both of these verb forms are just part of a verb phrase and need a helper to be included in the S-V-C. You can also remember that the word *participle* derives from "participate" and that a participle "takes part" in a sentence in various ways.

With a regular verb, both the simple past (she *walked*) and the past participle (she *has walked*) are alike. For that reason, it's not possible to identify the past participle of a regular verb unless you see it in a sentence. Note how the word *walked* acts as both simple past and past participle in the following sentences.

- We <u>walked</u> and <u>walked</u>. (simple past)

- We <u>had walked</u> for miles. (past participle, active voice)

- The dog <u>was walked</u> by its master. (past participle, passive voice)

Participles as Adjectives

Now, see how a change of word order varies the function of the participles in the following sentences.

- The masterpiece was stolen.
  (S-V) [The] masterpiece/was stolen

- The police returned the masterpiece to its owner.
  (S-V-C) [The] police/returned/[the] masterpiece.

- The police returned the *stolen* masterpiece.

Presto! The participle is now taking part in the sentence as an adjective, yet it still carries the idea of action. Both past and present participles, when used as adjectives, can easily be seen as carrying the idea of a simple sentence.

Identify the participles that function as adjectives in the following sentences.

1. The crying baby wants attention. _____

2. We might as well throw away that broken transistor radio.

_____

3. An imagined monster can be almost as fearsome as a real one.

_____

4. A familiar adage is "A watched pot never boils."

_____

Answers: 1. crying 2. broken 3. imagined 4. watched

Participial Phrases

Just as a participle can work alone as an adjective, so can a **participial phrase,** which consists of a participle plus its modifiers and complements.

- <u>Coming back from California,</u> we stopped for a few days in Las Vegas.
- I am wearing a ring <u>given to me by my great-aunt.</u>

Coming back from California and *given to me by my great-aunt* are participial phrases. It helps to think of a participial phrase as a former sentence with its subject and helping verbs chopped off so it can be combined with another clause. By adding these missing words, the sentence *I am wearing a ring given to me by my great-aunt* can be broken into these two sentences:

- I am wearing a ring.
- The ring was given to me by my great-aunt.

What ring? (One that was) <u>given to me by my great-aunt.</u> The entire phrase works as an adjective. Both *to me* and *by my great-aunt* are prepositional phrases modifying *given.*

Because a participle also has qualities of a verb, it can do what ordinary adjectives can't. It can have an object, as these examples show.

- Jenny <u>was showing</u> her sense of humor.
  (S-V-C) Jenny/was showing/sense
- Jenny did not take the remark seriously.
  (S-V-C) Jenny/did take/[the] remark
- <u>Showing her sense of humor,</u> Jenny did not take the remark seriously.

Yes, *sense* is still an object in the last sentence.

Identify the participles and participial phrases working as adjectives, as well as the nouns or pronouns they modify.

1. Printed in red, the manuscript hurt my eyes.

2. His smiling face hid his wounded pride.

TIP

When can an adjective take an object? Only when it's a word, such as a participle, that can also work as a verb. Even when it serves as an adjective, a present or past participle can still have objects and its own modifiers, just as it does when it's part of a verb phrase.

3. The clouds, driven by the wind, were a sign of the changing weather.

4. A coded message held the secret of the missing treasure.

5. Anyone knowing the truth would question the company's boasting claims about the product.

6. Wearing that color, you look exceptionally attractive.

7. No one ever recovered the money stolen in the robbery.

Participles or Participial Phrases	Word Modified
1. _____	_____
_____	_____
2. _____	_____
_____	_____
3. _____	_____
_____	_____
4. _____	_____
_____	_____
5. _____	_____
_____	_____
6. _____	_____
_____	_____
7. _____	_____

Answers: 1. Printed in red/manuscript 2. smiling/face; wounded/pride 3. driven by the wind/clouds; changing/weather 4. coded/message; missing/treasure 5. knowing the truth/anyone; boasting/claims 6. Wearing that color/you 7. stolen in the robbery/money

TIP

Don't ask a participial phrase to modify a possessive.

- (faulty) <u>Jumping up,</u> Ozzie's reaction was instant.
   (S-V-C) reaction/was/ instant
      A reaction can't jump.
- (correct) <u>Jumping up,</u> Ozzie reacted instantly.

AVOID DANGLING AND MISPLACED PARTICIPLES

When a word is missing or a participle is carelessly placed, confusion results. See how the same phrase can alter a sentence's meaning when moved to a different position.

- <u>Flying to California,</u> we saw the Grand Canyon.
- We saw the Grand Canyon, <u>flying to California.</u>
- <u>Flying to California,</u> the Grand Canyon was seen.

The last two sentences make it seem that the Grand Canyon was flying. Because of the importance of word order, readers rightfully assume that participial phrases are meant to describe whatever noun or pronoun is nearest. Don't be guilty of dangling or misplacing a participle. The result sounds silly, and many consider it a serious crime against good grammar.

THE GERUND: ANOTHER VERSATILE VERBAL

Identify the part of speech of the underlined words in the following sentence.

- <u>Sailing,</u> <u>swimming,</u> and <u>waterskiing</u> are popular water sports.

Without a second thought, most people would say that *sailing, swimming,* and *waterskiing* are nouns. Of course, they'd be right. Together, they make up the compound subject of the sentence.

But notice the *-ing* endings. Although they're often taken for granted, such nouns are also verb forms that can be used with helping verbs, as in "The ship is sailing." All can serve as adjectives, too, as in "sailing ship," "swimming expert," and "waterskiing enthusiast." Only the *-ing* form of the participle can work as a noun; when it does, it's called a **gerund.**

What's the difference between a gerund and a present participle? In the way they look, none at all. You can only tell when they are at work. Notice how present participles express action in the following verb phrases:

- First arrivals <u>will be coming</u> soon.
   (S-V) arrivals/will be coming

- They <u>have been doing</u> the job carefully.
  (S-V-C) They/have been doing/[the] job

- I <u>am keeping</u> a journal.
  (S-V-C) I/am keeping/[a] journal

> **TIP**
>
> Double-check a gerund by testing another noun or pronoun in its place.

Compare them with the following, which have the same form, but are now called gerunds.

- Thank you for <u>coming</u>.

- <u>Doing the job carefully</u> can often save time in the long run.

- You should start <u>keeping a journal</u>.

> **TIP**
>
> The *-ing* form of the verb, which expresses an action in progress, is the only verb form that works as a noun, or gerund.

Gerunds or gerund phrases will always answer the noun question, *what?* (Since they name an action, they don't answer to *who?*) In the first example, *coming* is an object of a preposition. In the second, *Doing the job carefully,* the entire gerund phrase, is the subject; and in the third, *keeping a journal* is the direct object.

Being verbals, gerunds do not only work as nouns. They can also have objects and be modified by adverbs and adverb phrases. In the preceding examples, *carefully* is an adverb modifying *Doing,* and both *Doing* and *keeping* have direct objects.

A Fine Point of Using Gerunds

Because a gerund is a noun, a possessive noun, formed with an apostrophe or possessive form of the pronoun, should be used to show possession.

- <u>Being tired</u> can cause carelessness.

- <u>Bill's being tired</u> caused his carelessness. (Bill's, not Bill)

- *His* <u>being tired</u> caused his carelessness. (his, not him) *Bill's* modifies the gerund subject, <u>being tired</u>.

The gerund could, of course, be turned into a participial phrase:

- <u>Being tired</u>, Bill was careless.

As sentences become more complicated, it's even more important to remember the first step in grammar: Know the Subject-Verb-Complement.

Identify the past and present participles at work in the following sentences. Some sentences contain more than one verbal. In the blank spaces, write the word or phrase and whether it is used as part of the verb phrase, as an adjective, or as a gerund. If it is a gerund, indicate whether it serves as a subject, direct object, or object of a preposition, etc.

• Being sure of the S-V-C will make the job easier!
  (S-V-C) Being sure/will make/[the] job

1. We are having trouble with our old car.

2. Keeping it in working order is almost a full-time job.

3. We have been thinking of selling the rattling old collection of scrap metal.

4. You could almost pity the poor old thing, broken down by many miles of driving.

5. In a joking way, we sometimes talk of retiring it.

6. Judging by its resale value, the worthless thing deserves being junked.

7. Loved by no one, wanted by no one, our old car is facing a future as dim as its failing headlights.

Verb or Verbal Phrase	Use in Sentence
1. _____	_____
2. _____	_____
3. _____	_____
_____	_____
4. _____	_____
_____	_____
5. _____	_____
_____	_____

Verb or Verbal Phrase	Use in Sentence
6. _____	_____
_____	_____
7. _____	_____
_____	_____
_____	_____

Answers: 1. are having/verb phrase 2. Keeping it in working order/gerund phrase/subj. adj. 3. have been thinking/verb phrase; selling the . . . scrap metal/gerund phrase/obj. prep.; rattling/adj. 4. broken down . . . of driving/adj. phrase; driving/gerund/obj. prep. 5. joking/adj.; retiring it/gerund phrase/obj. prep. 6. judging by its resale value/adj. phrase; being junked/gerund phrase/dir. obj. 7. Loved by no one, wanted by no one/adj. phrases; is facing/verb phrase; failing/adj.

TO BE OR NOT TO BE: THE INFINITIVE

The **infinitive** is known as the simple form of the verb—simply because it doesn't express the notion of tense or time. In English, *to* is the sign of the infinitive, but you should not confuse it with the preposition *to*.

To the store is a prepositional phrase that works as an adjective or adverb. *To go* is an infinitive, with the *to* acting as part of a whole. The infinitive is the most versatile of verbals, for it's able to work as a noun, an adjective, and even as an adverb.

Noun: <u>To go</u> seemed impossible. (subject)

Adjective: That's the place <u>to go</u>.

Adverb: We were waiting <u>to go</u>.

As do other verbal phrases, an infinitive phrase can include objects and adverbial modifiers:

- We hope <u>to go early in the morning</u>.
  To go when? <u>early</u> (adverb)
  To go when? <u>in the morning</u> (prepositional phrase, used as adverb)

The infinitive can also have a subject, but the subject of the infinitive is in the objective case:

- The boss expects me <u>to prepare a report on our sales prospects</u>.

To get a better understanding of how infinitives work, compare the following pairs of sentences. See how infinitives can serve as various parts of speech.

Infinitives as Nouns

- They want a <u>house</u> in the country.
  (S-V-C) They/want/[a] house

- They want <u>to buy a house in the country</u>.

The entire infinitive phrase, *to buy a house in the country,* is the object of the verb, *want. House* is the direct object of the infinitive, *to buy.*

- Do you expect a <u>miracle</u>?
  (S-V-C) you/do expect/[a] miracle

- Do you expect <u>me to perform a miracle</u>?
  me to perform a miracle = object of the verb, *expect*
  me = subject of the infinitive, *to perform*
  miracle = the object of *to perform*

Infinitives as Adjectives

- The horse <u>in the lead</u> is Swift Eagle.
  (S-V-C) horse/is/Swift Eagle

- The horse <u>to watch</u> is Swift Eagle.
  in the lead = prepositional phrase, adjective
  to watch = infinitive, adjective

- This is the car stereo <u>for you</u>.
  (S-V-C) This/is/[the] stereo

- This is the only car stereo <u>to feature such high quality at a low price</u>.

Infinitives as Adverbs

- We stayed up <u>late</u>.
  (S-V) We/stayed

- We stayed up <u>to watch the late news</u>.
  to watch the late news = infinitive phrase, adverb

- The guard patrolled the gate <u>constantly</u>.

- The guard patrolled the gate <u>to prevent outsiders from entering</u>.

A Few Verbs Allow Infinitives to Work Without To

- The wind made the curtains <u>flutter</u>.

- Do you hear him <u>sing</u>?

- We will let them <u>help</u>.

Change the verb *made* to *cause, did hear* to *did ask,* and *let* to *allow.* See how the sign of the infinitive, *to,* appears naturally. Of course, you could also say: A few verbs let infinitives work without *to.*
  And infinitives, like other verbals serving as modifiers, can dangle!

- (faulty) <u>To speak frankly</u>, that color is not flattering to you.
  Can a color speak frankly?

- (correct) <u>To speak frankly</u>, I think that color is really you.

THE EXPLETIVE *IT*: THE SECRET IS KNOWING THE RIGHT QUESTIONS

The word *it* often begins a sentence that contains an infinitive used as a predicate nominative or as the true subject. In this case the word *it* is not a true pronoun but simply an introductory word, called an **expletive.**

- It is my ambition <u>to be a lawyer</u>.

To determine whether *it* is a pronoun or expletive, ask "What is the subject of the sentence? Who or what is the sentence about?" In this case, the answer is *my ambition,* which is therefore the subject.

- My ambition is <u>to be a lawyer</u>.

  Then, *to be a lawyer* is a predicate noun. In this case, the word *it* doesn't really take the place of a noun nor have a complement, and so is an expletive. Here is another example.

- It takes time <u>to do good work</u>.

• To do good work takes time.

The subject is *to do good work*; *it* is an expletive.

There has a similar use as an expletive in sentences. For example: *There* is reason to be thankful. (See the discussion of *there* as an expletive on pages 108–109.)

GRAMMAR TO THE RESCUE

Grammar is a way of discovering how language works best. It's not a way of forcing language to do anything. English is ever-expanding and ever-changing. It's becoming simpler in some ways and more complicated in others.

It's not always necessary to worry about the more obscure details of grammar. Gerunds, participles, and infinitives have baffled many. Consider yourself lucky if they make complete sense to you.

Don't make yourself work at grammar; make grammar work for you. Have as your first goal to find the subject/verb. If you do, you'll always know what's really happening in any sentence.

SELF-TEST

1. In the following sentences, identify the S-V-Cs. Then, pick out the infinitive phrases, and decide if they are used as nouns, adjectives, or adverbs. If the infinitive works as a noun, determine its specific use in the sentence: subject (s), direct object (d.o.), or subjective complement (s-c).

   a. The team tried to make the short yardage by rushing.

   b. Lou was hurrying to be there on time.

   c. I would like a gift to please someone very special.

   d. It makes me happy to hear so much applause.

   e. To like oneself is important.

   f. A child needs someone to be a role model.

   g. We have been waiting to hear the judges' decision.

   h. Her dream has always been to travel in space.

	S-V-C or S-V	Infinitive Phrase	Type	Use, If Noun
a.	_____	_____	_____	_____
b.	_____	_____	_____	_____

	S-V-C or S-V	Infinitive Phrase	Type	Use, If Noun
c.	_____	_____	___	_____
d.	_____	_____	___	_____
e.	_____	_____	___	_____
f.	_____	_____	___	_____
g.	_____	_____	___	_____
h.	_____	_____	___	_____

ANSWERS

a. (S-V-C) (The) team/tried/to make . . . yardage; to make the short yardage/n./d.o. b. (S-V) Lou/was hurrying; to be there on time/adv. c. (S-V-C) I/would like/gift; to please someone very special/adj. d. (S-V-C) To hear . . . /makes/me; To hear . . . applause/n./s. e. (S-V-C) To like . . . /is/important; to like oneself/n./s. f. (S-V-C) Child/needs/someone; to be . . . model/ adj. g. (S-V) We/have been waiting; to hear the judges' decision/adv. h. (S-V-C) dream/has been/to travel in space; to travel in space/pred. noun

2. The following sentences contain faulty elements, which include dangling participles and infinitives, as well as improperly modified gerund phrases. Write a corrected version of those that contain an error. If a sentence is correct, simply identify it as such.

   a. Looking toward the west, threatening clouds loomed. _____

   _____

   b. To tell the truth, his idea seems impractical. _____

   _____

   c. Him liking Shakespeare is a real surprise to me. _____

   _____

   d. Josh stared at the mischievous puppy, smiling in disbelief. _____

   _____

   e. To become better acquainted, the meeting will include a social hour. _____

   _____

f. What to you think of Jill planning to become a doctor? _____

_____

g. Spoken in a quiet but firm voice, her words rang as the truth. ____

_____

h. Broken down for the umpteenth time, I decided my car repair bills were getting out of hand. _____

_____

i. Found by an honest person, Eric told us his lost credit card has been returned. _____

_____

ANSWERS

Possible answers: a. Looking toward the west, we saw threatening clouds looming. b. To tell the truth, I think his idea seems impractical. c. His liking Shakespeare is a real surprise to me. d. Smiling in disbelief, Josh stared at the mischievous puppy. e. The meeting will include a social hour so those attending can become better acquainted. f. What do you think of Jill's planning to become a doctor? g. Correct. h. After my car broke down for the umpteenth time, I decided my repair bills were getting out of hand. i. Eric told us an honest person had found and returned his lost credit card.

16

More Punctuation: I Said, "May I Have Your Attention, Please?"

Punctuation is an attention-getting device. Yet its purpose is not to call attention to itself but to clarify the sense of sentences and paragraphs.

Capitalization works in much the same way. Both capital letters and punctuation should help carry a message along more smoothly and clearly, not cause road bumps or confusion. When punctuation is correct, you probably aren't even aware of it.

PUNCTUATION HELPS MAKE SENTENCES CLEAR

what would it be like without punctuation marks or capital letters it would be terrible the reader would have to puzzle out when a sentence or complete thought ended no one would know for sure whether the cowboys were a group of range riders or a football team they might think sixty minutes was a period of time instead of a television program

the problems go on but theres no way to stop without a period.

QUOTATION MARKS

Quotation marks are used to call attention to something "different" in a sentence. Their most frequent use is to surround the exact words that someone is saying, has said, or has written in the type of sentence called a **direct quotation.**

Understanding how quotation marks work can help you become both a better writer and reader.

The two elements of a direct quotation are

1. Something said:

- "It's too bad that you must leave so soon."

- "Are you sure you must go?"

2. Someone saying it, plus, of course, a bit more punctuation.

Quotations allow plenty of room for variety. Identification of the speaker, also called **attribution,** can come first, set off by a comma. End punctuation of the quoted words comes within the quotation marks.

- Davina said, "It's too bad that you must leave so soon."

- Davina asked, "Are you sure you must go?"

Or identification can come at the end.

- "It's too bad that you must leave so soon," Davina said.

- "Are you sure you must go?" asked Davina.

Note that a single quoted statement needs only a comma, then quotation marks before the identification. The only period goes at the end of the whole sentence. A quoted question or exclamation requires its own question or exclamation mark inside quotation marks and no comma after.

Identification can also be placed in the middle of a quotation.

- "It's too bad," said Davina, "that you must leave so soon."

- "Are you sure," she asked, "that you must go?"

In the middle of a sentence, the identification is set off by commas. Notice their placement in relation to the quotation marks that signal when the quote stops and then begins again. Since the second half of the quote does not begin a sentence, it does not begin with a capital letter.

Two or more quoted sentences can be included inside a single pair of quotation marks.

- "It's too bad that you must leave so soon. Are you sure you must go?" Davina asked.

Or they may share a single identification but be punctuated separately.

- "It's too bad that you must leave so soon," said Davina. "Are you sure you must go?"

Notice how the first sentence ends with a period after *Davina,* and the following sentence stands by itself in the paragraph.

Of course, the identification can have its own modifiers:

- The girl in the trench coat shrugged and said doubtfully, "Well, if you say so."

Unless other words are necessary, good writers stick to just plain *said,* not *whispered, shouted,* or *gasped.* After all, the important part of a quotation is usually the quoted words, not how they are said.

Rewrite the following sentences with quotation marks and other necessary punctuation and capitalization.

1. Wade said I hope you understand my point of view

   _____

   _____

2. Please give me one more chance Bert begged

   _____

   _____

3. Dan declared I need more time to think

   _____

   _____

4. What are you doing asked Alice

   _____

   _____

5. I am on my hands and knees explained Ed to look for my lost button

   _____

   _____

6. His actions confused me too replied Ruth

_____

_____

7. Just listen to my side of the story Paul pleaded

_____

_____

8. Ted told Terry you have the wrong idea

_____

_____

9. Look out cried Cathy you're going to run into that door

_____

_____

10. Someone watching observed Otis wouldn't understand this at all

_____

_____

Answers: 1. Wade said, "I hope you understand my point of view." 2. "Please give me one more chance," Bert begged. 3. Dan declared, "I need more time to think." 4. "What are you doing?" asked Alice. 5. "I am on my hands and knees," explained Ed, "to look for my lost button." 6. "His actions confused me, too," replied Ruth. 7. "Just listen to my side of the story," Paul pleaded. 8. Ted told Terry, "You have the wrong idea." 9. "Look out!" cried Cathy. "You're going to run into that door!" 10. "Someone watching," observed Otis, "wouldn't understand this at all."

Reading Dialogue

As you read, keep in mind the following uses of quotation marks in paragraphs of written dialogue.

1. A new paragraph should begin each time there is a change of speaker.

2. Once in a while, the speaker will remain the same for more than one paragraph. If so, the quotation mark will be missing at the end of all but the last paragraph, although quotation marks will begin each one.

Example:

> "This was not what I expected," said Brynn. "If I had known you would take it this way, I would never have invited the Benningtons to attend, but I thought it would be a good way to get you two together again.
>   "After all, you were good friends for so long. Oh . . . please, don't go!"

A quotation mark at the end of the paragraph means the end of the speech. Charles Dickens in *A Tale of Two Cities* uses an entire chapter to quote a man's story of his time in solitary confinement. The chapter opens with a quotation mark—each paragraph starts with one, too—but only at the end of the chapter does the closing quotation mark come.

3. The good reader concentrates on the conversation and only checks the identification to make sure who is speaking.

4. Identification is often left out completely when it's clear who is speaking. When just two people are speaking, each new paragraph, if surrounded by quotation marks, signals a switch in speaker.

Quotation Marks in Action

Here is a sample of John Steinbeck's masterful use of dialogue. Steinbeck reveals what his characters are like by letting them speak for themselves. In this selection from *Of Mice and Men,* George is trying to keep Lennie from saying something to spoil their chances of getting jobs as ranch hands.

Notice Steinbeck's use of quotation marks, identification, and paragraphing to make the course of conversation clear.

> . . . The boss licked his pencil. "What's your name?"
> "George Milton."
> "And what's yours?"
> George said, "His name's Lennie Small."
> The names were entered in the book. "Le's see, this is the twentieth, noon the twentieth." He closed the book. "Where you boys been working?"
> "Up around Weed," said George.
> "You, too?" to Lennie.
> "Yeah, him too," said George.
> The boss pointed a playful finger at Lennie. "He ain't much of a talker, is he?"
> "No, he ain't, but he's sure a hell of a good worker. Strong as a bull."

Lennie smiled to himself. "Strong as a bull," he repeated.

George scowled at him, and Lennie dropped his head in shame at having forgotten.

The boss said suddenly, "Listen, Small!" Lennie raised his head. "What can you do?"

In a panic, Lennie looked at George for help. "He can do anything you tell him," said George. "He's a good skinner. He can rassel grain bags, drive a cultivator. He can do anything. Just give him a try."

The boss turned on George. "Then why don't you let him answer?"

More Ways Quotation Marks are Used

Quotations marks have other special uses, besides setting off dialogue. Use them to enclose titles of short pieces: short stories, poems, articles, chapters, and so on.

- Have you read "Sea Lullaby" by Elinor Wylie?

Use them to set off words used in a special way in order to call attention to them or explain them and to enclose definitions.

- Modern technology has adopted many familiar words, such as "surf" and "crash," to suit its needs.

- Why are writers like James Fenimore Cooper "hard" to read?

- *Quidnunc means* "a gossip or busybody."

ITALIC LETTERS

Italics are correct for the following uses, although underlining often takes the place of italics in handwritten material and some printed matter.

1. Italics set off the titles of books and other long works.

    - *The Grapes of Wrath* by John Steinbeck makes the suffering of migrant workers come to life.

    - Cher won an Oscar for her role in *Moonstruck*.

2. Italics are used for foreign words and phrases.

    - Judd considers himself a *bon vivant*.

3. Italics highlight words used as words, not carrying their usual meaning.

- When spoken, sound-alikes such as *there, their,* and *they're* are impossible to tell apart unless used in a sentence.

THE COLON

Use a colon after a statement introducing a list, explanation, illustration, or the like.

- In grammar always remember to do the following first: Find the subject/verb.

Note: Do not use a colon to introduce words that complete a statement and are themselves part of the subject/verb/complement.

- (incorrect) The three essentials of good manners are: respect, consideration, and understanding. (The words following *are* belong to the statement as its complement.)

- (correct) Remember the three essentials of good manners: respect, consideration, and understanding.

A CHANGING APPROACH TO LANGUAGE

Compare the following two sentences. Each is from page 312 of a novel by a well-known American author, one of the past and one of the present. Each is the opening sentence of its paragraph. First, James Fenimore Cooper, from *The Deerslayer,* written in 1859.

As soon as the light was sufficiently strong to allow of a distinct view of the lake, and more particularly of its shores, Hutter turned the head of the ark directly toward the castle, with the avowed intention of taking possession for the day at least, as the place more favorable for meeting his daughters and for carrying on his operations against the Indians.

Then, Toni Morrison, from *Paradise,* published in 1998.

Sally Albright, walking north on Calumet, stopped suddenly in front of the plate glass windows of Jennie's Country Inn.

Picked at random from the works of two widely read American authors, the two sentences show the difference between writers of the past and present. Today's writers use much shorter sentences. The longest sentence written by Morrison on her page 312 has twenty-one words. Cooper's longest has sixty-four. Cooper's shortest sentence has seventeen words. Morrison's shortest sentences have two words, and there are four of this length. Morrison's sentences have an average of 7.38 words. Cooper's are over five times as long, with an average of 40.15 words.

Why is a writer like Cooper considered hard to read? Most people would probably guess that he used a difficult vocabulary; actually, more problems arise from his sentence length. That's what really makes the going hard for someone who doesn't understand how grammar works and as a result gets lost in a long sentence.

Cooper, like all able writers, knew the importance of using shorter words, prepositions, and conjunctions to direct the reader to the strong words (nouns and verbs) that answer the important questions. Yet readers often feel lost because they don't understand how grammar works.

Can you spot the Subject-Verb of Morrison's nineteen-word sentence?

(S-V) Sally Albright/stopped

What about the main Subject-Verb-Complement of Cooper's sixty-four-word sentence?

(S-V-C) Hutter/turned/[the]head

What head? <u>of the ark</u>

When? <u>as soon as the light was sufficiently strong</u>

Where? <u>directly toward the castle</u>

Why? <u>with the avowed intention of taking possession</u>

. . . and so on

Here is how Cooper's sentence would sound if it had been written as a series of simple sentences.

> Soon the light was sufficiently strong. It allowed a distinct view of the lake. It more particularly gave a good view of its shores. Hutter turned the ark. He headed directly toward the castle. He intended to take possession of it. He meant to hold it for the day at least. It was a place more favorable for meeting his daughters. It was also better for carrying on his operations against the Indians.

Is this an improvement? Using shorter sentences does take a few more words. The important question is, "Does it carry the same meaning?"

In addition to following the rules of grammar, both writers have their own style. In part it's a reflection of their times, and it's also a reflection of their own voices. At first, a writer's style may seem difficult to read, but after a few paragraphs or pages, you begin to feel the natural rhythm in which that writer speaks.

SELF-TEST

TIP

How you use punctuation depends largely on what you are writing and who your audience will be. Follow the traditional rules of punctuation for formal writing. It's still important to know the rules—so you will know what effect you want to achieve, when and if you choose to break them.

Rewrite the following sentences, supplying correct punctuation. Pay particular attention to the use of quotation marks, colons, and italics. (You may wish to review other rules of punctuation in chatper 11.)

1. The Sun Also Rises is one of Ernest Hemingway's best-known novels

   _____

2. Remember the first step Read the instructions

   _____

3. There is no doubt said Kyle that the time has come to take a stand

   _____

4. One sense of the word spin is to tell only what twists a situation to your own advantage

   _____

5. Have you noticed any changes asked Lanie

   _____

6. After I read The Necklace I realized why it is considered one of the greatest short stories ever written

   _____

7. What pain a foolish mistake can cause Jed said

   _____

8. Amigo is the Spanish word for a male friend while amiga means a female friend

   _____

ANSWERS

1. *The Sun Also Rises* is one of Ernest Hemingway's best-known novels.
2. Remember the first step: Read the instructions. (A period after *step* is also correct.)
3. "There is no doubt," said Kyle, "that the time has come to take a stand."
4. One sense of the word *spin* is to tell only what twists a situation to your own advantage.
5. "Have you noticed any changes?" asked Lanie.
6. After I read "The Necklace," I realized why it is considered one of the greatest short stories ever written.
7. "What pain a foolish mistake can cause!" Jed said.
8. *Amigo* is the Spanish word for a male friend, while *amiga* means a female friend.

17 Combining Sentences

Understanding grammar includes knowing how parts of sentences fit together. The two short sentences below are **simple sentences.** They may also be called **independent clauses** because they can stand alone. The first has a subject/verb/complement. The second has just subject/verb.

- I expect a reply.

- Two weeks have passed.

The simplest way of joining these two is in a **compound sentence,** using *and, or, but, for,* or a semicolon, as in the following example.

- I expect a reply, and two weeks have passed.

As far as grammar goes, the compound sentence follows a formula. Two or more independent clauses + a coordinating conjunction to join them = a compound sentence. However, in this case, the two clauses, joined by *and,* work no better together than they did alone.

WHAT MAKES A SENTENCE COMPLEX

A different set of words, called **subordinating conjunctions,** are used in **complex sentences.** Here are three examples:

- I expect a reply <u>because</u> two weeks have passed.

- I expect a reply <u>when</u> two weeks have passed.

- I expect a reply <u>after</u> two weeks have passed.

What has happened? The underlined words, each a subordinating conjunction, change the way the clauses work together and make them complex sentences. Now, "I expect a reply" has become the more important of the two clauses. The second clause simply answers *why* or *when* about the other's verb, *expect*. It has become a dependent clause with the entire clause working as an adverb.

This is the formula for forming a complex sentence:

an independent clause + one or more
dependent clauses = a complex sentence

In a complex sentence, the subordinating conjunction is the key, for it always counts as part of the dependent clause it introduces. It shows how two clauses are related and how one affects the other's meaning. Subordinating conjunctions have this name because they place their clause in a position under, or subordinate to, a main clause. Don't forget to include the conjunction when identifying a dependent clause.

There are three types of dependent clauses, classed by whether they work as adverbs, adjectives, or nouns.

> **TIP**
>
> Subordinate clause is another name for dependent clause.

THE ADVERB CLAUSE

Here is a list of words often used as subordinating conjunctions in adverb clauses, along with the questions they most nearly seem to answer.

WHEN?	WHY?	HOW?	WHERE?
after	because	as if	where
as	if	however	wherever
as soon as	in case	provided	
before	so that	than	
since	unless		
till	although*		
until	though*		
when			
while			

(*conveys a negative sense)

Don't forget that many of these words can also work in other ways in a sentence. You must see them in action to be sure.

In each of the following sentences, identify the main clause, the dependent clause, and the S-V-C. Underline the subordinating conjunction. Don't forget that this kind of conjunction is part of its clause because of its importance to the meaning.

1. We have not heard from Chet since he left for Europe.

2. You usually find loads of unexpected information when you surf the Internet.

3. Fran plays tennis as if she gets plenty of practice.

4. The new system saves time because it combines two steps into one.

5. You often find a missing object where you least expect it to be.

1. Main Clause _____ (S-V) _____

    Adv. Clause _____ (S-V) _____

2. Main Clause _____ (S-V-C) _____

    Adv. Clause _____ (S-V-C) _____

3. Main Clause _____ (S-V-C) _____

    Adv. Clause _____ (S-V-C) _____

4. Main Clause _____ (S-V-C) _____

    Adv. Clause _____ (S-V-C) _____

5. Main Clause _____ (S-V-C) _____

    Adv. Clause _____ (S-V-C) _____

Answers: 1. We have not heard from Chet; (S-V) We/have [not] heard
                <u>since</u> he left for Europe; (S-V) he/left
           2. You usually find . . . information; (S-V-C) you/find/loads
                <u>when</u> you surf the Internet; (S-V-C-) you/surf/Internet
           3. Fran plays tennis; (S-V-C) Fran/plays/tennis
                <u>as if</u> she gets plenty of practice; (S-V-C) she/gets/plenty
           4. The new system saves time; (S-V-C) system/saves/time
                <u>because</u> it combines two steps into one; (S-V-C) it/combines/steps
           5. You often find . . . object; (S-V-C) you/find/object
                <u>where</u> you least expect it to be; (S-V-C) you/expect/it

Punctuating Adverb Clauses

Complex sentences with adverb clauses can be written in either natural or transposed order. In **natural order** the main clause comes first, followed by the dependent clause, and no comma need separate them.

- I was in a state of shock when I saw Gina with her new hair style.

In **transposed order,** a dependent clause precedes the main clause. A comma is needed to separate the two clauses, as in the example below.

- When I saw Gina with her new hair style, I was in a state of shock.

Follow the same style of punctuation for complex sentences having more than one adverb clause, as illustrated by the following examples.

- I have been waiting since the office opened because I have an important question for Mr. Richardson.

    Main Clause: (S-V) I/have been waiting

    Adverb Clause 1: since the office opened

       (S-V) [the] office/opened (*since* tells when.)

    Adverb Clause 2: because I have . . . Richardson

       (S-V-C) I/have/question (*because* tells why.)

- Because I have an important question for Mr. Richardson, I have been waiting since the office opened.

Asking the Right Questions

An adverb clause can also modify a verbal working as a noun, adjective, or adverb. Remember, verbals have split personalities; they can work as various parts of speech but they always keep some qualities of a verb.

- I wanted to speak with you as soon as you came in.

    (S-V-C) I/wanted/to speak with you
    to speak with you = infinitive phrase, used as direct object
    to speak when? as soon as you came in. (S-V) you/came

THE MAIN CLAUSE

The essential requirement of any sentence is a main clause that can stand alone as a sentence.

● Coming into the dazzling sunlight, I could not see clearly until my eyes adjusted.

Main Clause: (S-V) I/ could [not] see
Adverb Clause: until my eyes adjusted
(S-V) eyes/adjusted (*until* tells when)
Participial Phrase: coming into the dazzling sunlight

I could not see would be a perfectly good sentence all by itself. Without this main clause, the sentence would not be complete.

In the following sentences, first, pick out the main clause and its S-V-C. Next, identify the adverb clause or clauses and the S-V-C of each. Determine what each modifies and what question it answers.

1. Sandy picked at her eggplant as if she didn't really like it.

2. You can't be sure about a dish until you have tried it.

3. Since squid sounds unappetizing to me, I will only try a small bit of it.

4. Being a very fussy eater, Carol can find little to please her when she eats at fast-food restaurants.

5. After you finish, you will enjoy a piece of key lime pie if you have room for dessert.

6. I will meet you wherever you say and whenever the time is convenient for you.

7. We will be working on the project until Monday because many details need testing before the prototype is okayed.

1. Main Clause _____ (S-V-C) _____
   Adv. Clause _____ (S-V-C) _____

2. Main Clause _____ (S-V-C) _____
   Adv. Clause _____ (S-V-C) _____

3. Main Clause _____ (S-V-C) _____

Adv. Clause _____ (S-V-C) _____

4. Main Clause _____ (S-V-C) _____

Adv. Clause _____ (S-V-C) _____

5. Main Clause _____ (S-V-C) _____

Adv. Clause _____ (S-V-C) _____

Adv. Clause _____ (S-V-C) _____

6. Main Clause _____ (S-V-C) _____

Adv. Clause _____ (S-V-C) _____

Adv. Clause _____ (S-V-C) _____

7. Main Clause _____ (S-V-C) _____

Adv. Clause _____ (S-V-C) _____

Adv. Clause _____ (S-V-C) _____

Answers: 1. main clause: Sandy picked at her eggplant (S-V) Sandy/picked; adv. clause: as if she didn't really like it (S-V-C) she/did[n't] like/it; picked/how? 2. main clause: You can't . . . a dish (S-V-C) you/can[n't] be/sure; adv. clause: until you have tried it (S-V-C) you/have tried/it; can[n't] be sure/when? 3. main clause: I will only . . . of it (S-V-C) I/will try/bit; adv. clause: Since squid . . . to me (S-V-C) squid/ sounds/unappetizing; will [not] try/why? 4. main clause: Being a fussy . . . her (S-V-C) Carol/can find/little; adv. clause: when she eats at fast food restaurants (S-V) she/eats; can find/when?; participial phrase: being a very fussy eater 5. main clause: you will enjoy . . . pie (S-V-C) you/will enjoy/piece; adv. clauses: After you finish (S-V) you/finish; will enjoy/when?; if you have . . . dessert (S-V-C) you/have/ room; will enjoy/when? 6. main clause: I will meet you (S-V-C) I/will meet/you; adv. clauses: wherever you say (S-V) you/say; will meet/where?; whenever . . . for you (S-V-C) time/is convenient; will meet/when? 7. main clause: We will be . . . until Monday (S-V) We/will be working; adv. clauses: because many details need testing (S-V-C) details/need/testing; will be working/why?; before the prototype is okayed (S-V-C) prototype/is/okayed; need/when?

THE ADJECTIVE CLAUSE

What is the best way to combine the following two sentences?

- Ben is an old friend.

- Ben comes from my hometown, Pittsfield.

None of the adverbial conjunctions fit well, nor would forming a compound sentence help. The solution lies in the word *Ben* used in both sentences. The best way to combine them is to form a dependent adjective clause that describes the word *Ben* in the main clause.

- Ben is an old friend <u>who comes from my hometown, Pittsfield.</u>

What happens in an adjective clause? The S-V of the second original sentence is

(S-V) Ben/comes

As a dependent clause, it changes to

(S-V) who/comes

In an adjective clause, a word such as *who* does double duty. It does not simply join two clauses, but takes an active part in its own clause. Here, of course, *who* is the subject. Words that work like *who* are called **relative pronouns.**

Relative pronouns have two functions in a complex sentence.

1. Relative pronouns form an adjective clause by attaching themselves, or relating, to a noun or pronoun in another clause.

2. They also have a definite role to play in their own clauses, as subject, direct object, object of a preposition, and so on.

Words commonly used as relative pronouns include:

- who, whom (reserved for persons)
- which (for things, including animals and places)
- that (for persons and things)

There are also compound forms, including *whoever, whomever,* and *whichever.* Remember, words that serve as relative pronouns can do other work in a sentence, such as introduce a question.

In the following pair of sentences, *suggestion* is the word that makes it possible to combine them into a single complex sentence with an adjective clause. First, identify the S-V-C of each.

- The boss liked the suggestion.
  (S-V-C) (The) boss/liked/[the] suggestion

- Joyce made the suggestion to him.
  (S-V-C) Joyce/made/[the] suggestion

Now combine the two as a complex sentence with adjective clause.

- The boss liked the suggestion <u>that Joyce made to him.</u>

What is the S-V-C of the dependent clause?
  (S-V-C) Joyce/made/that

The word *that* acts as both direct object and relative pronoun. The relative pronoun jumps to the head of the clause to attach itself to the noun, which it renames, and which the entire adjective clause modifies. Did you spot the adjective clauses that are used in this paragraph?

- which it renames

- which the entire adjective clause modifies

- that are used in this paragraph

Who and Whom

Consider the following related sentences:

- Matt is an electrical engineer.
  (S-V-C) Matt/is/[an] engineer

- I recently met Matt.
  (S-V-C) I/met/Matt

These simple sentences may be combined two ways, depending on which clause you wish to be the main one.

- I recently met Matt, <u>who is an electrical engineer.</u>

- Matt is an electrical engineer <u>whom I met recently.</u>

Why use *whom* instead of *who* in the second example? If you put a pronoun in the place of Matt, the reason will be clear.

- He is an electrical engineer.
  He = *who,* used as relative pronouns in the nominative case

- I recently met him.
  him = *whom,* used as relative pronouns in the objective case

Here is an illustration of the importance of word order. You can also highlight Matt as an individual, not as a member of a profession.

- Matt, <u>whom I recently met</u>, is an electrical engineer.

Remember that two sentences combined through the use of an adjective clause must both contain the same noun or a noun and its pronoun replacement.

Essential and Nonessential Clauses

Consider the following short, simple sentences.

- Trent is someone.

- I know him well.

Trent is <u>someone</u>? The sentence has a working S-V-C (Trent/is/someone), yet it sounds incomplete. Then, what about one of these?

- Trent is someone <u>that I know well</u>.

- Trent is someone <u>whom I know well</u>.

As a relative pronoun, *that* should introduce only essential adjective clauses, those that are necessary to identify or describe a noun in a sentence such as "Trent is someone."

Adjective clauses using *which, who* or *whom* may or may not be essential, depending upon their meaning. If a clause is nonessential, use a comma or pair of commas to set it off from the rest of the sentence.

- Bill Stoddard, <u>who graduated in 1997</u>, holds the school's scoring record.

- I finally received Terri's letter, <u>which I was awaiting eagerly</u>.

- We are pleased with the work of Jed McBride, <u>whom Mr. Leland hired last week</u>.

   If adjective clauses are essential, show this by not setting them off with commas. Remember, the use of the relative pronoun *that* always indicates that an adjective clause is essential. Use of commas to set off adjective clauses joined by other relative pronouns depends upon their sense and the writer's intention.

- A student <u>who graduated in 1998</u> holds the high jump record. (Essential)

- I finally received the letter <u>that Terry promised to write</u>. (Essential)

- We are pleased with the work of the new man <u>whom Mr. Leland hired</u>. (Comma depends upon the need for identification.)

- The company and union reached a decision <u>which should satisfy both sides</u>.

Relative Adverbs

Relative adverbs can also introduce adjective clauses.

- The day <u>when we met</u> was the happiest of my life.
   (S-V-C) [The] day/was/[the] happiest
   What day? <u>when we met</u>
   (S-V) we/met

   When not only modifies *met* but also connects the entire adjective clause to the subject of the main clause, *day*. Notice the part that word order plays here, too. Relative adverbs and adjectives come at the beginning of adjective clauses, which follow the noun or pronoun they describe.

   Here are more words working as relative adverbs.

- The weeks <u>since</u> you left have seemed like years.

- Clark plans to return to Utah, <u>where</u> he was born.

- Older people often love to tell of the days <u>when</u> they were younger.

Notice that adverbs answering *when* and *where* attach adjective clauses to nouns that name times and places.

Words that can work as relative adverbs include *after, before, since, when, where, while,* and *why*. When is a word a relative adverb, and when is it a subordinate conjunction? It all depends on what question the clause answers. It can be confusing.

- We vacationed at the lake <u>where our friends own a cottage</u>.
  (S-V) We/vacationed
  At what lake? <u>where our friends own a cottage</u> (an adjective clause with *where* as a relative adverb)

- Many astronauts have gone <u>where no man has ever gone before</u>.
  (S-V) astronauts/have gone
  Have gone where? <u>where no man has ever gone before</u> (Since the dependent clause gives the correct answer, it must be an adverb clause.)

It's not a crime that deserves hanging to confuse an adjective clause with an adverb clause. But it is important to identify the main clause and its subject/verb. This is what the sentence is all about. Dependent clauses simply answer questions about the main clause.

Whose: A Relative Adjective

The word *whose,* called a **relative adjective,** can also introduce an adjective clause.

- I admire the paintings of Monet, <u>whose work is being exhibited at the museum</u>.

Whose modifies *work;* its entire clause modifes *Monet.*

- Nick finally met the composer <u>in whose honor the party was given.</u>

Whose modifes *honor.* The party was given in his (whose) honor. Note that the word order changes and the relative adjective comes after the preposition. This avoids the awkwardness of breaking up the prepositional phrase. (Nick finally met the composer whose honor the party was given in.)

In the following sentences, first find the main clause and its S-V-C. Then identify each adjective clause and list the noun or pronoun that it modifies. Label each adjective clause as essential or nonessential. Some sentences have more than one adjective clause.

1. Mark enjoys any kind of music that has a good beat.

2. All of the people whom I asked agree about the new ruling, which went into effect last week.

3. Marian has a new kitten, which she named Beeper.

4. Do you remember the time when you locked yourself out of your apartment?

5. The novel that I just finished will not satisfy anyone who prefers a happy ending.

1. Main Clause _____ (S-V-C) _____

    Adj. Clause _____ (Word Mod.) _____

2. Main Clause _____ (S-V-C) _____

    Adj. Clause _____ (Word Mod.) _____

    Adj. Clause _____ (Word Mod.) _____

3. Main Clause _____ (S-V-C) _____

    Adj. Clause _____ (Word Mod.) _____

4. Main Clause _____ (S-V-C) _____

    Adj. Clause _____ (Word Mod.) _____

5. Main Clause _____ (S-V-C) _____

    Adj. Clause _____ (Word Mod.) _____

    Adj. Clause _____ (Word Mod.) _____

Answers: 1. main clause: Mark . . . music (S-V-C) Mark/enjoys/kind; adj. clause: that has a good beat/music; essential 2. main clause: All . . . ruling (S-V) All/agree; adj. clauses: whom I asked/people; essential; which went into effect last week/ ruling; nonessential 3. main clause: Marian . . . kitten (S-V-C) Marian/has/kitten; adj. clause: which she named Beeper/kitten; nonessential 4. main clause: Do you . . . time (S-V-C) you/do remember/time; adj. clause: when you locked . . . apart-ment/time; essential 5. main clause: The novel . . . anyone (S-V-C) novel/will [not] satisfy/anyone; adj. clauses: that I just finished/novel; essential; who prefers a happy ending/anyone; essential

Combine the following pairs of simple sentences into complex sentences with adjective clauses. For some, there is more than one possible answer.

1. The director called extra rehearsals. He is a perfectionist.

    _____

2. The joke has a punch line. I don't find it funny.

    _____

3. Mr. Carlson is considered an authority on the Civil War. Mr. Carlson is a retired army officer.

    _____

4. The company president was accused of embezzlement. Everyone had trusted the company president.

    _____

5. Carla is a natural leader. She rarely loses her temper.

    _____

Answers: 1. The director, who is a perfectionist, called extra rehearsals. 2. The joke has a punch line that I don't find funny. 3. Mr. Carlson, who is considered an authority on the Civil War, is a retired army officer.—or—Mr. Carlson, who is a retired army officer, is considered an authority on the Civil War. 4. The company president, whom everyone had trusted, was accused of embezzlement.—or—Everyone had trusted the company president, who was accused of embezzlement. 5. Carla, who rarely loses her temper, is a natural leader.—or—Carla is a natural leader who rarely loses her temper. (There are also other possible answers.)

FORMING COMPLEX SENTENCES

Once you know how adjective and adverb clauses work, you can put them together and separate them all you wish. The essential ingredient is always a main clause that can stand alone. Then you can add

- one or more adverb clauses
- one or more adjective clauses
- an adjective clause attached to a word in an adjective clause
- verbals

as long as the main clause is clear!

- Before I moved to Michigan, I lived in North Carolina, which is a state that does not have such extreme variations in weather.

  Main Clause   = I lived in North Carolina

  Adverb Clause   = Before I moved to Michigan

  Adjective Clause = which is a state

  Adjective Clause = that does not have such extreme variations in weather

Remember, a main clause can sound silly or incomplete when an essential adjective clause is missing.

- Because I was unprepared for Michigan weather, I did not expect summer temperatures that reached 95 degrees and higher.
  (S-V-C) I/did [not] expect/temperatures

This main clause needs its essential adjective clause, *that reached 95 degrees and higher,* to sound complete.

In the following sentences, find the main clause and its S-V-C, identify the dependent clauses, and decide whether the dependent clauses are adjective or adverb clauses, judging by the questions they answer and what they modify.

1. When we came into the ski lodge, we warmed ourselves by the fireplace.

2. We first attempted the beginners' slope, which seemed difficult enough to me.

3. Before we left for the ski resort, I bought an outfit that looked perfect for a pro.

4. The moment before I started downhill was a time when I fervently wished to be somewhere else.

5. Although I tried not to show my fear, the instructor recognized me as someone who was on the verge of panic.

6. When I reached the bottom of the slope, which had seemed so steep, I looked back up toward the top.

7. The slope where I first tried skiing will always be a mountain to me, even though my friends call it a molehill.

1. Main Clause ＿＿＿＿＿＿＿ (S-V-C)   ＿＿＿＿＿＿＿
   Dep. Clause ＿＿＿＿＿＿＿ Adv. or Adj. ＿＿＿＿＿＿＿

2. Main Clause ＿＿＿＿＿＿＿ (S-V-C)   ＿＿＿＿＿＿＿
   Dep. Clause ＿＿＿＿＿＿＿ Adv. or Adj. ＿＿＿＿＿＿＿

3. Main Clause ＿＿＿＿＿＿＿ (S-V-C)   ＿＿＿＿＿＿＿
   Dep. Clause ＿＿＿＿＿＿＿ Adv. or Adj. ＿＿＿＿＿＿＿
   Dep. Clause ＿＿＿＿＿＿＿ Adv. or Adj. ＿＿＿＿＿＿＿

4. Main Clause ＿＿＿＿＿＿＿ (S-V-C)   ＿＿＿＿＿＿＿
   Dep. Clause ＿＿＿＿＿＿＿ Adv. or Adj. ＿＿＿＿＿＿＿
   Dep. Clause ＿＿＿＿＿＿＿ Adv. or Adj. ＿＿＿＿＿＿＿
   Dep. Clause ＿＿＿＿＿＿＿ Adv. or Adj. ＿＿＿＿＿＿＿

5. Main Clause ＿＿＿＿＿＿＿ (S-V-C)   ＿＿＿＿＿＿＿
   Dep. Clause ＿＿＿＿＿＿＿ Adv. or Adj. ＿＿＿＿＿＿＿
   Dep. Clause ＿＿＿＿＿＿＿ Adv. or Adj. ＿＿＿＿＿＿＿

6. Main Clause ＿＿＿＿＿＿＿ (S-V-C)   ＿＿＿＿＿＿＿
   Dep. Clause ＿＿＿＿＿＿＿ Adv. or Adj. ＿＿＿＿＿＿＿
   Dep. Clause ＿＿＿＿＿＿＿ Adv. or Adj. ＿＿＿＿＿＿＿

7. Main Clause ＿＿＿＿＿＿＿ (S-V-C)   ＿＿＿＿＿＿＿
   Dep. Clause ＿＿＿＿＿＿＿ Adv. or Adj. ＿＿＿＿＿＿＿
   Dep. Clause ＿＿＿＿＿＿＿ Adv. or Adj. ＿＿＿＿＿＿＿

Answers: 1. main clause: we warmed . . . fireplace (S-V-C) we/warmed/ourselves; dep. clause: When we came into the ski lodge; adverb/*when?* 2. main clause: We first . . . slope (S-V-C) we/attempted/slope; dep. clause: which seemed difficult enough to me; adjective/slope 3. main clause: I bought . . . outfit (S-V-C) (I/bought/outfit; dep. clauses: Before we left for the ski resort; adverb/*when?*; that looked perfect for a pro; adjective/outfit 4. main clause: The moment . . . time (S-V-C) moment/was/time; dep. clauses: before I started downhill; adjective/moment; when I fervently wished to be somewhere else; adjective/time 5. main clause: the instructor . . . someone, (S-V-C) instructor/recognized/me; dep. clauses: Although I tried not to show my fear; adverb/negative *how?*; who was full of panic; adjective/ someone 6. main clause: I looked . . . top (S-V) I/looked; dep. clauses: When I reached the bottom of the slope; adverb/*when?*; which had seemed so steep; adjective/slope 7. main clause: The slope . . . to me (S-V-C) slope/will be/mountain; dep. clauses: where I first tried skiing; adjective/slope; even though my friends call it a molehill; adverb/(negative) *why?*

<table>
<tr><td>

TIP

Remember, words can have multiple functions. To know a word's part of speech, first check to see what work it does in a sentence. Words such as *after, before, since,* and *until* can work many ways in sentences: as prepositions, adverbs, subordinate conjunctions, relative adverbs, and even adjectives.

</td><td>

Test yourself on the following *before* and *after* sentences, illustrating the different uses of these two words. See if you can identify their part of speech in each italicized use, and write your answer in the blank space. Some are tricky; remember the questions to ask.

1. We left for the airport *before* dawn. _____

2. I had never flown by helicopter *before*. _____

3. Justine arrived in Washington on the day *before* the conference officially began. _____

4. She watched herself on videotape *before* she felt ready to give her speech at the convention. _____

5. *After* the speech there was a question-and-answer period. _____

6. *After* the applause ended, Justine felt tired but happy. _____

7. Often the morning *after* is unpleasant, but this one spelled relief. _____

Answers: 1. preposition 2. adverb 3. relative adverb 4. subordinating conjunction 5. preposition 6. subordinating conjunction 7. adjective

</td></tr>
</table>

THE NOUN CLAUSE

The noun clause is probably the most difficult kind of dependent clause to identify. It shows the importance of asking the right question—and believing the answer.

- I know the <u>answer</u>.

- I know <u>who will win</u>.
  (S-V-C) I/know/_____ /_____

Know what? In the first example, it's the noun *answer.* In the second, it is *who will win,* which has an S-V of its own: who/will win. Like the word *answer,* it is used as the direct object of *know.* As a statement, *who will win* can't stand alone. It is a dependent clause, used as a single part of speech in the sentence. It's a **noun clause.**

Separating a noun clause from its main clause can be tricky because it is often an integral part of the whole.

A noun clause can do anything, or almost anything, a noun can. It can act as a subject:

- His <u>words</u> puzzled me.
  (S-V-C) words/puzzled/me

- <u>What he said</u> puzzled me.
  (S-V-C) What he said/puzzled/me

It can act as a direct object:

- I don't know their <u>address</u>.

- I don't know <u>where they live</u>.

It can act as a predicate nominative:

- The choice should be <u>yours</u>.

- The choice should be <u>whichever you like best</u>.

It can act as an object of a preposition:

- His appearance was different from my mental <u>image</u> of him.

- His appearance was different from <u>what I imagined</u>.

Or even as an object of an infinitive:

- I'd like to understand Thad's <u>viewpoints</u>.

- I'd like to understand <u>how Thad thinks</u>.

It can also act as an indirect object:

- You can give <u>visitors</u> the schedule of events.

- You can give <u>whoever wants one</u> the schedule of events.

Or a retained object:

- I was asked my <u>opinion</u> of the President's action.

- I was asked <u>what I thought</u> of the President's action.

It can even act as an appositive:

- I will tell you the truth, the plain <u>facts</u>.

- I will tell you the truth, <u>that we are broke</u>.

Noun clauses work like any other words or phrases used as nouns. They answer the noun question, *what?* They often express a quality of indefiniteness or doubt. Noun clauses can also relate to a process. They don't directly answer the question, *who?*

What Makes Noun Clauses Difficult?

A noun clause is almost always part of the main clause, which usually doesn't make complete sense without it. A noun clause can even belong to the heart of a main clause and be its subject or complement. The connecting word may or may not be part of it.

Words Often Introducing Noun Clauses
Pronouns: who, whom, which, what, that, whoever, whomever, whichever
    (*Which, what, that,* etc., may also be used as introductory adjectives in noun clauses.)
Adverbs: how, where, why, if, whether, when
The word *that* is sometimes used as a conjunction, merely to join a noun clause to the rest of its sentence.

- I know <u>that you are right</u>.
  (S-V-C) I/know/that you are right

Note: *That* is often left out and understood.

- I know <u>you are right</u>.
  (S-V-C) I/know/you are right

Working With Noun Clauses

Begin with a simple sentence.

- I know your <u>name</u>.
  (S-V-C) I/know/name

Turn it into a complex sentence by replacing the noun *name* with a noun clause.

- I know <u>what you want</u>.
  (S-V-C) I/know/who you are
  (Noun clause S-V-C) you/want/what
  What is a direct object within its clause.

- I know <u>why you came</u>.
  (Noun clause S-V) you/came
  Why is an adverb within its clause.

- I know <u>who she is</u>.
  (Noun clause S-V-C) she/is/who
  Who is a predicate nominative in its clause.

- I know <u>whom you saw</u>.
  (Noun clause S-V-C) you/saw/whom
  Whom is the direct object of *saw*.

- I know <u>that can't be true</u>.
  (Noun clause S-V-C) that/can [not] be/true
  That is the subject of the noun clause.

- I know <u>that story is true</u>.
  (Noun clause S-V-C) story/is/true
  Story is the subject; *that,* its adjective.

- I know <u>that it is true</u>.
  (Noun clause S-V-C) it/is/true
  That is a conjunction; you could just as well say, "I know it is true."

To know how noun clauses work, as with everything in grammar, you just need to ask the right questions.

In complex sentences, noun clauses often work to allow the delay or qualification of a piece of information. In the following examples, note how both sentences are introduced by observations concerning the statements made in the noun clauses.

- It is amazing <u>how fast gossip travels</u>.
  (S-V-C) how fast gossip travels/is/amazing

It is an introductory word, an expletive. The noun clause is the true subject.

- I don't know <u>why Charley didn't tell me first</u>.
  (S-V-C) I/do[n't] know/why Charley didn't tell me first

Noun Clauses in Questions
Remember, questions are often in transposed order. This is especially true of questions containing noun clauses.

- <u>Who</u> do you think <u>is most talented</u>?
  (S-V-C) you/do think/who is most talented
  (Noun clause S-V) who/is/talented

- <u>Whom</u> do you think <u>he will choose</u>?
  (S-V-C) you/do think/ he will choose whom
  (Noun clause S-V-C) he/will choose/whom

Making the right choice between pronouns such as *I/me, she/her, he/him, we/us, they/them,* and *who/whom* is another fine point that shows you understand how grammar works.

In the following sentences, first, spot the main S-V-C. Remember that a noun clause can work as the subject or complement of the main clause. List the part of speech for which each noun clause is used in its sentence. Watch for a sentence having more than one noun clause.

1. I understand why Hubie felt embarrassed.

2. Whoever calls can leave a message.

3. Some people never want what is best for them.

4. Your birthday cake will be whatever flavor you like.

5. I have been thinking about what you told me.

6. Tell whomever you call how important the meeting is.

7. Where Sparky has gone is anyone's guess.

TIP
Choose a pronoun because of its actual work in its own clause, not from its place at the beginning of a sentence. When you are speaking it's sometimes hard to know at the outset exactly where your sentence will end, so it's easy to make a mistake. But when you write, always check to make sure which pronoun is really needed.

	Main S-V-C	Noun Clause	Pt. of Speech
1.	_____	_____	_____
2.	_____	_____	_____
3.	_____	_____	_____
4.	_____	_____	_____
5.	_____	_____	_____
6.	_____	_____	_____
		_____	_____
7.	_____	_____	_____

Answers: 1. (S-V-C) I/understand/why . . . embarrassed; noun clause: why Hubie felt embarrassed/direct object 2. (S-V-C) Whoever calls/can leave/message; noun clause: whoever calls/subject 3. (S-V-C) people/want/what . . . them; noun clause: what is best for them/direct object 4. (S-V-C) cake/will be/whatever . . . like; noun clause: whatever flavor you like/predicate nominative 5. (S-V) I/have been thinking; noun clause: what you told me/object of a preposition 6. (S-V-C) [You]/tell/how . . . is; noun clauses: whomever you call/indirect object; how important the meeting is/direct object 7. (S-V-C) Where . . . gone/is/guess; noun clause: where Sparky has gone/subject

SELF-TEST

Underline the dependent clause in each of the following sentences, and identify its type: noun, adjective, or adverb. Then, if a noun clause, name its case use: subject, direct object, etc. If an adjective or adverb clause, name the word it modifies.

1. After several hours had passed, we decided to wait no longer.

2. A police officer directed traffic at the busy intersection because the stoplight was out.

3. Jeremy is someone who likes to play practical jokes.

4. Nobody knows what he'll do next.

5. When he is around, you can always expect surprises.

6. Most people have secrets that they wish no one else to know.

7. A friend whom you can trust is a friend indeed.

8. That his theory might be wrong never occurred to him.

9. From what she hinted, I guessed the truth.

	Type	Case Use or Word Modified		Type	Case Use or Word Modified
1.	_____	_____	2.	_____	_____
3.	_____	_____	4.	_____	_____
5.	_____	_____	6.	_____	_____
7.	_____	_____	8.	_____	_____
9.	_____	_____			

ANSWERS

1. <u>After several hours had passed</u>, we decided to wait no longer.; adv./decided 2. A police officer directed traffic at the busy intersection <u>because the stoplight was out</u>.; adv./directed 3. Jeremy is someone <u>who likes to play practical jokes.</u>; adj./someone 4. Nobody knows <u>what he'll do next.</u>; noun/dir. obj. 5. <u>When he is around</u>, you can always expect surprises.; adv./can expect 6. Most people have secrets <u>that they wish no one else to know.</u>; adj./secrets 7. A friend <u>whom you can trust</u> is a friend indeed.; adj./friend 8. <u>That his theory might be wrong</u> never occurred to him.; noun/subj. 9. From <u>what she hinted</u> I guessed the truth.; noun/obj. of prep.

18 Keeping It Simple, Even When Sentences Get Complex

Remember the process of building sentences?
A simple sentence:

> The family spent its vacation in Mexico.

A simple sentence with compound predicate:

> They enjoyed the sights and loved the Mexican people.

A compound sentence:

> Tortillas are the order of the day, and the Mexicans know countless ways to serve them.

A complex sentence:

> If you go to Mexico, you can practice your skills at bargaining in the colorful markets.

And even a compound-complex sentence:

> When you come home, you can show people your souvenirs and photos, but nothing compares with actually being there.

Then you can add any number of verbals: infinitives, gerunds, and participles. . . .
In English, you can put sentence parts together and scramble them up in endless combinations.

WHAT GOOD IS A COMPLEX SENTENCE?

English is basically a word-order language. A simple sentence states a simple, direct thought.

- Baby wants a cookie.

A verbal adds a new idea.

- Baby wants mother to bring him a cookie.

A dependent clause adds another.

- Baby wants mother to bring him one of the chocolate cookies that she bought at the supermarket yesterday.

And there's more to the situation that will make the sentence compound.

- Baby wants mother to bring him one of the chocolate cookies that she bought at the supermarket yesterday, or baby will cry.

Why? One more dependent clause will explain.

- Baby wants mother to bring him one of the chocolate cookies that she bought at the supermarket yesterday, or baby will cry because that usually gets fast results.

Is a complex sentence better than a simple sentence? It all depends upon what needs to be said.

In many ways a complex sentence does more work than a simple one. It organizes ideas and ties them together. It can show what is more important than something else. It can show cause and effect because it makes clear how one thing depends upon another.

A complex sentence sometimes makes life easier because it can indicate the relative importance of clauses and thereby help clarify a complicated idea. But beware of someone who uses fancy grammar just to impress and to dress up a dull, unoriginal idea; it happens more often than you might think.

A simple idea often calls for a simple sentence—a complex idea, a complex one.

THE SOUND OF LANGUAGE

Good writers know that language also contains sound and rhythm. This is part of how grammar and word order work. A good writer knows that verbals and dependent clauses and conjunctions help carry the reader along. They make the key words, the nouns and verbs, ring out and proclaim their importance.

The Writer at Work

Following is a rewritten version of two paragraphs from F. Scott Fitzgerald's *The Great Gatsby,* revised into simple sentences. They describe a fabulous party taking place at Gatsby's mansion during Prohibition, the Jazz Age.

By seven o'clock the orchestra has arrived. It is no thin, five-piece affair. There is a whole pitful of oboes, trombones, saxophones, viols, cornets, piccolos, and low and high drums. The last swimmers have come in from the beach now. They are dressing upstairs. The cars from New York are parked five deep in the drive. Already the halls, salons, and verandas are gaudy with primary colors. Girls wear their hair shorn in strange new ways. Their shawls are colorful beyond the dreams of Castille. The bar is in full swing. Floating rounds of cocktails permeate the garden outside. The air is alive with chatter, laughter, casual innuendo, and introductions. They are all forgotten on the spot. There are enthusiastic meetings between women. They never knew each other's names.

The lights grow brighter. The earth lurches away from the sun. Now the orchestra is playing yellow cocktail music. The opera of voices pitches a key higher. Laughter is easier minute by minute. It is spilled with prodigality. It is tipped out at a cheerful word. The groups change more swiftly. They swell with new arrivals. They dissolve and form in the same breath. Already there are wanderers. Confident girls weave here and there among the stouter and more stable. They become for a sharp, joyous moment the center of a group. Then they become excited with triumph. They glide on through the sea-change of faces, voices, and color. The light also is constantly changing.

Now see how Fitzgerald uses not only phrases and clauses but also words like *and* to bring the picture of the party together. Compare the two versions to see how the simple sentences fit within his longer ones. By knowing how grammar works, Fitzgerald makes his sentences also carry the idea of the combining and changing and moving in which the people at the party are engaging.

By seven o'clock the orchestra has arrived, no thin five-piece affair, but a whole pitful of oboes, trombones, saxophones, viols, cornets, piccolos, and low and high drums. The last swimmers have come in from the beach now and are dressing upstairs. The cars from New York are parked five deep in the drive, and already the halls, salons, and verandas are gaudy with primary colors, and hair shorn in strange new ways, and shawls beyond the dreams of Castille. The bar is in full swing, and floating rounds of cocktails permeate the garden outside, until the air is alive with chatter, laughter, casual innuendo, and introductions forgotten on the spot, and enthusiastic meetings between women who never knew each other's names.

The lights grow brighter as the earth lurches away from the sun, and now the orchestra is playing yellow cocktail music, and the opera of voices pitches a key higher. Laughter is easier minute by minute, spilled with prodigality, tipped out at a cheerful word. The groups change more swiftly, swell with new arrivals, dissolve and form in the same breath; already there are wanderers, confident girls who weave here and there among the stouter and more stable, become for a sharp, joyous moment the center of a group, and then, excited with triumph, glide on through the sea-change of faces and voices and color under the constantly changing light.

To be good with language, you need an ear for its music as well as a knowledge of its system of grammar. Good grammar and good writing are not necessarily the same thing.

GRAMMAR IN ACTION

Accomplished writers will create sentences that may be difficult to analyze. When you read, try to be aware of the simple sentences that lie within the more complex forms. You do not need to know exactly how every word and phrase works, just as you do not need to know the meaning of every word in order to grasp what you read.

In fact, reading is an excellent way to increase your vocabulary as well as extend you knowledge.

Keep in mind the simple sentences that Charles Dickens combines to create the following picture of an English town he calls Coketown. It is from his novel *Hard Times,* in which a schoolmaster called Gradgrind claims, "In this life, we want nothing but Facts, sir; nothing but Facts."

As you are reading, note the simple sentences that join together to form the compound and complex ones. Also, notice repeated words, such as *like,* with which Dickens calls attention to what he considers important.

Coketown, a city dedicated to facts, is as dull as its school.

It was a town of red brick, or of brick that would have been red if the smoke and ashes had allowed it; but as matters stood it was a town of unnatural red and black like the painted face of a savage. It was a town of machinery and tall chimneys, out of which interminable serpents of smoke trailed themselves forever and ever, and never got uncoiled. It had a black canal in it, and a river that ran purple with ill-smelling dye, and vast piles of buildings full of windows where there was a rattling and trembling all day long, and where the piston of the steam-engine worked monotonously up and down like the head of an elephant in a state of melancholy madness. It contained several large streets all very like one another, and many small streets still more like one another, inhabited by people equally like one another, who all went in and out at the same hours, with the same sound upon the same pavements, to do the same work, and to whom every day was the same as yesterday and tomorrow, and every year the counterpart of the last and the next.

. . . You saw nothing in Coketown but what was severely workful.

A sentence should be as long or as short as it needs to be. The only requirement is that its parts join together and depend upon one another clearly and correctly. It can never be too short or too long if it says what it needs to say.

WHAT MAKES GRAMMAR IMPORTANT?

Here's what Robert Claiborne wrote in *Our Marvelous Native Tongue*. Read it both for ideas and for an understanding of how another writer combines sentences.

If, in 1700, you were chatting with another resident of your native town or village, understanding was no problem: both of you would almost certainly use the same syntax, acquired in childhood, and any unclarity of meaning could be quickly resolved by asking, "What do you mean?" The writer preparing his copy for the printer was in quite a different situation: he was addressing himself to people he had never seen and in all likelihood never would see. If they found his syntax obscure, they could not cross-question him, but would likely damn him for an ignoramus and resolve never to read him again.

And, on the same subject, Daniel J. Boorstin wrote in *The Discoverers*:

After Gutenberg (1454), realms of everyday life once ruled and served by Memory would be governed by the printed page. In the late Middle

Ages, for the small literate class, manuscript books had provided an aid, and sometimes a substitute, for Memory. But the printed book was far more portable, more accurate, more convenient to refer to, and of course, more public. Whatever was in print, after being written by an author, was also known to printers, proofreaders, and anyone reached by the printed page. A man could now refer to the rules of grammar. . . .

Whether writing about grammar or expertly using it, these writers show the true importance of knowing how grammar works.

SELF-TEST

Below is a paragraph from *Out of Africa,* in which Isak Dinesen tells of her experiences as manager of a coffee plantation in Kenya. To discover the effectiveness of complex sentences, rewrite the following paragraph as a series of simple sentences. Use each underlined verb or verb phrase as the main verb of a separate sentence. You may need to supply words, omit them, or change their form, as necessary.

Out on the Safaris, I <u>had seen</u> a herd of Buffalo, one hundred and twenty-nine of them, <u>come</u> out of the morning mist under a copper sky, one by one. . . . I <u>had seen</u> a herd of Elephant <u>travelling</u> through dense Native forest, where the light <u>is strewn</u> down between the thick creepers in small spots and patches, <u>pacing</u> along as if they <u>had</u> an appointment at the end of the world. . . . I <u>had followed</u> two Rhinos on their morning promenade, when they <u>were sniffing and snorting</u> in the air of the dawn,— which <u>is</u> so cold it <u>hurts</u> in the nose,—and <u>looked</u> liked two very big angular stones <u>rollicking</u> in the long valley and <u>enjoying</u> life together. . . .

1. _____

2. _____

3. _____

4. _____

5. _____

6. _____

7. _____

8. _____

9. _____

10. _____

11. _____

12. _____

13. _____

14. _____

ANSWERS

1. Out on the Safaris, I had seen a herd of Buffalo. 2. One hundred and twenty-nine of them had come out of the morning mist under a copper sky, one by one. 3. I had seen a herd of Elephant. 4. They were travelling through dense Native forest. 5. There the light is down between the thick creepers in small spots and patches. 6. The elephants were pacing along. 7. They seemed to have an appointment at the end of the world. 8. I had followed two Rhinos on their morning promenade. 9. They were sniffing and snorting in the air of the dawn. 10. The dawn air is so cold. 11. It hurts in the nose. 12. The rhinos looked liked two very big angular stones. 13. The rhinos were rollicking in the long valley. 14. They were enjoying life together.

19 Verbs Do More: The Fine Points of Using Verbs

Working with verbs proves that verbs do more than express the idea of an action or the act of being. Verbs never just lie there; they always take an active part in a sentence. Here is a review of what verbs do:

1. Verbs express time or tense, such as

   Present: I <u>see</u>
   Past: I <u>saw</u>

2. Verbs also have voice.

   Active: I <u>see</u>
   Passive: I <u>was seen</u>

3. Verbs may change to express number.

   Third Person Singular: She (he, it) <u>sees</u>.
   Other Persons: I (you, we, they) <u>see</u>.

4. Verbs may act on objects or act alone. Some work both ways.

   Intransitive: We <u>see</u>.
   Transitive: We <u>see</u> someone.

5. Verbs help direct the purpose of a sentence.

   Statement: You <u>see</u>.
   Question: <u>Do</u> you <u>see</u>?

Command: <u>See</u>.

Exclamation: How well you <u>see</u>!

VERBS ALSO HAVE MOODS

In grammar, there's no such thing as a good or bad mood. **Mood** simply means the attitude of the speaker toward the words being spoken. English has three moods: indicative, imperative, and subjunctive. You've already seen two of them at work to help indicate a speaker's purpose.

Indicative: The Most Common Mood

In any tense or voice, **indicative** is the mood that shows or points out that the verb is simply dealing with actual data. Most statements, questions, and exclamations use the indicative mood.

- <u>Do</u> you <u>like</u> soap operas?
- I <u>can't say</u> that I do.

Obviously, these are indicative.

- A three-headed monster <u>ate</u> my brother-in-law.
- What a struggle that <u>must have been</u>!

These, too, are indicative. The indicative mood does not mean a sentence must be taken seriously or accepted as fact. It means that its chief aim is simply to convey its meaning. It is the mood used for the ordinary expression of most statements and questions.

Imperative: The Mood That Commands

The **imperative** mood is used for giving commands.

- <u>Listen</u> here.
- <u>Be</u> happy.
- <u>Don't</u> <u>waste</u> a second!
- <u>Try</u> to be both strong and gentle, firm and loving.

The imperative is the base form of the verb used with a "you understood" subject. It expresses an order or direct request to do as the speaker commands.

Subjunctive: The Mood of Possibilities

The **subjunctive** mood uses an out-of-the-ordinary verb form to call attention to something extraordinary.

- How I wish I <u>were</u> back home!

But *I were* is never correct, is it? (I am, I was, I will be, I . . . We were, you were, they were, . . . never *I were*.)

Yet that's how the subjunctive mood works. It uses an unexpected verb form, one that's incorrect in ordinary usage, to call attention to the fact that it's saying something unusual. It deals in possibilities, desires, things supposed, not known, often contrary to fact. In the sentence above, *I were* makes it clear that the speaker, *I,* is not at home.

To signal that the subjunctive is at work, these are the basic changes:

- <u>was</u> to <u>were</u>
  I wish that were so. (contrary to fact)

- <u>am, is, are</u> to <u>be</u>
  If that be true, we must act soon. (possibility)

- dropping the final *s* from the *-s* form of the third person singular (she <u>sees</u> to she <u>see</u>)

Like a number of other precise old forms of language, the subjunctive is also disappearing from common use. One reason is that English often uses a different helper instead of making actual changes in the verb itself. This can achieve a similar effect without truly using the subjunctive mood. Yet many people who care about language are still listening, and paying attention to the subjunctive mood is another way to show respect for the tools of language.

Here's where and how the subjunctive still makes a difference.

1. **The subjunctive expresses a condition contrary to fact.** Compare the following sentences.

   - If I <u>were</u> a big lottery winner, I would quit working.

   - If I <u>win</u> the lottery, I will quit working.

   - I <u>was</u> a big lottery winner, so I quit working.

Of course, the first example illustrates the subjunctive in action. The word *subjunctive* also contains the idea of being "under," or subordinate to, another idea. In the first example, the subjunctive is used in a dependent clause that expresses something contrary to fact that would take place with respect to the main verb in the clause. It's an adverb clause, answering the question *why?*

Notice how the main clause of the first example uses the helping verb *would,* which also shows it's just a possibility. Both the second and third examples are in the indicative mood. In the third example, *was* expresses a fact, in contrast to the condition contrary to fact in the first example.

All three of the following dependent clauses are in the subjunctive mood.

- Mike would have more friends if he <u>were</u> not so conceited.

- If I <u>were</u> taller, this dress might look better.

- If you <u>were</u> I, what would you do?

Notice that *you were* is no different from the indicative form. Along with *they, we,* and other plural nouns and pronouns, a verb having *you* as its subject doesn't change in the subjunctive. One reason the subjunctive is disappearing is that it's not always evident. Sometimes you must simply know it's there.

2. **The subjunctive mood expresses a neutral condition or strong doubt.**

- If the rumor <u>were</u> true, what does that mean for the future?

- If there <u>be</u> any justice, we will win the case.

- I enjoy all kinds of good music, whether it <u>be</u> classical or pop, symphonic or jazz.

3. **The subjunctive is used in noun clauses after wishes, orders, and firm requests.**

- I wish California <u>weren't</u> so far away from New York.

- I demanded that he <u>give</u> me the money.

- Her parents forbid that she <u>see</u> him again.

- I insist that you <u>be</u> quiet.

4. The subjunctive is used in a separate clause to express a deep desire.

- If only Tony <u>were</u> here!

- Would I <u>were</u> wrong!

- Heaven <u>help</u> us!

Note: Sometimes an *if* clause expresses a fact that the speaker hadn't known beforehand. In this case, the indicative mood is used.

- If Marta *was* home, why didn't she answer the phone?

In the following sentences, choose the word that properly expresses the subjunctive mood.

1. If there _____ more time, we could stop and see Drew. (was, were)

2. The director insists that everyone _____ on time for rehearsal. (be, is)

3. He tried to act as though he _____ not hurt by the thoughtless remark. (was, were)

4. Mr. Smith demanded that Tom _____ until the work was completed. (stay, stays)

5. I wish that Alex _____ here. (was, were)

6. The boss asks that the receptionist _____ all callers by their formal titles. (addresses, address)

7. If someone _____ to ask, I'd tell them that I think this project is a waste of time. (was, were)

Answers: 1. were 2. be 3. were 4. stay 5. were 6. address 7. were

COMMON VERBS THAT CAUSE UNCOMMON CONFUSION

Some of the most common verbs have sound-alike forms that are close in meaning but have important differences in their proper usage.

They are so often confused that only practice, careful listening, and determination to master their use will keep them separated. In each case, the difference is based on how they work in a sentence: whether they are transitive, requiring a direct object as complement, or intransitive, not needing one.

Transitive (with few exceptions)	Intransitive
lay (laid, laid, laying)	lie (lay, lain, lying)
• <u>Lay</u> the box there. (S-V-C) [you] lay/box	• The box <u>lies</u> on the floor. (S-V) box/lies
set (set, set, setting)	sit (sat, sat, sitting)
• She <u>set</u> her mind on winning. (S-V-C) she/set/mind	• The cat <u>sat</u> on the mat. (S-V) cat/sat
raise (raised, raised, raising)	rise (rose, risen, rising)
• The store <u>raised</u> its prices. (S-V-C) [The] store/ raised/prices	• The honoree <u>has risen</u> to speak (S-V) honoree/has risen

Is it *rise* or *raise*? *Sit* or *set*? *Lie* or *lay*? And how dare one *lay* be the past tense of *lie*, while the other has *lay, laid,* and *laid* as its principal parts? It seems almost cruel to mention the *lie* (*lied, lied, lying*) that means to tell a falsehood. No wonder these verbs are confusing—and a tricky test of someone's skill in grammar and usage.

Think of them as the transitive and intransitive trios.

The Transitive Trio: Lay, Set, Raise

A reasonable test for *lay, set,* and *raise* is to substitute a form of *put, place,* or *put in place* in its place. If it makes sense, you're right.

- I usually <u>lay</u> my sunglasses in the same place.
  (I put my sunglasses there.)

- I <u>set</u> the highchair in the corner, and then I <u>set</u> the baby in it.
  (I put the highchair in the corner, and then I put the baby in it.)

- I <u>raised</u> my hand.
  (I put up my hand.)

For each of the following sentences, list the subject/verb/complement. Be sure to include helping verbs.

1. We have set our hopes on a victory.

    _____

2. The fans in the stands raised their voices in unison for the school song.

    _____

3. The referee laid the ball on the one-yard line.

    _____

4. With one more touchdown pass, the quarterback will set a conference scoring record.

    _____

5. The coach is laying the groundwork for a surprise play.

    _____

6. Tomorrow, we will raise the victory banner to the top of the campus flagpole.

    _____

Answers: 1. we/have set/hopes 2. fans/raised/voices 3. referee/laid/ball 4. quarterback/will set/record 5. coach/is laying/groundwork 6. we/will raise/banner

The Intransitive Trio: Lie, Sit, Rise

Compare the previous three with the intransitive trio: _lie, sit, rise._ Remember things as well as people can _lie, sit,_ and _rise._

- I <u>lie</u> in bed late on Saturdays.

- A gum wrapper <u>lies</u> on the sidewalk.

- Gramps always <u>sits</u> in the same chair.

- The clock <u>sits</u> on the shelf.
  (Think of it as just resting there.)

- Gramps always <u>rises</u> at 6 a.m., no matter when the sun <u>rises</u>.
  (_Rise_ means to get up and go up.)

   For each clause in the following sentences, find the subject/verb. Being intransitive, verbs will not have complements. Pay attention to how the meaning determines the choice of verb. Watch for compound and complex sentences.

1. All morning long a fog lay over the countryside.

_____

2. Although the sun had risen, ghostly blobs of mist were still sitting close to the ground.

_____

3. A dog was lying in the yard.

_____

4. The farmer usually rose with the sun.

_____

5. An old, fallen tree trunk had lain across the creek for years.

_____

6. Two boys sat on the trunk, fishing, and another boy lay stretched out on his back.

_____

7. The water level was rising because of the recent rains.

_____

Answers: 1. fog/lay 2. sun/had risen 3. dog/was lying 4. farmer/rose 5. trunk/had lain 6. boys/sat; boy/lay 7. level/was rising

In each of the following sentences, choose the correct base form of the verb from the pair in parentheses. Check the helping verbs and complements to help you decide. Then fill in the blank with the form of this verb that fits both tense and meaning. If in doubt, check the chart at the beginning of this section.

1. Jodi Anderson has _____ to the top of her profession. (raise, rise)

2. The spices have _____ too long on the kitchen shelf. (set, sit)

3. Stu has _____ on the beach under the blazing sun for hours. (lay, lie)

4. Construction prices have been _____ recently. (raise, rise)

5. Will you _____ the report on top of that stack of papers? (set, sit)

6. Many papers are _____ in a jumble on the desk. (lay, lie)

7. Money for the trip was _____ by the team's supporters. (raise, rise)

8. On sleepless nights I have _____ awake for hours, listening to murmuring motors. (lay, lie)

9. The owners have _____ rust-colored outdoor carpet on their patio. (lay, lie)

10. The company president will _____ for a portrait. (set, sit)

Answers: 1. risen 2. sat 3. lain 4. rising 5. set 6. lying 7. raised 8. lain 9. laid 10. sit

More Common "Problem" Verbs

What's the problem with verbs like the following? It's choosing the right principle part of irregular verbs, such as those in the following list, to match the tense and voice of a sentence.

Root	Past	Past Participle	Present Participle
go	went	gone	going
do	did	done	doing
see	saw	seen	seeing
run	ran	run	running
come	came	come	coming

It's really a matter of usage, not meaning. Yet the wrong choice can prove distracting to those who know grammar. How do you choose the right principal part? To be sure, you need to understand how verbs work and to recognize the perfect tenses and passive voice.

As you fill in the blanks in the following exercise, check for tense and voice. Auxiliary verbs that signal use of the past participle include *has, have, had,* and *will have,* helpers of the perfect tenses, and forms of *be (is, was, has been,* etc.), helpers in the passive voice.

1. I would not have _____ without you. (go, went, gone)

2. What has that little rascal _____ now? (do, did, done)

3. As soon as Benny saw them coming, he _____ to tell his mother. (run, ran, run)

4. I had never _____ so far or fast in my life. (run, ran, run)

5. Sarah told us that she _____ everything that happened. (see, saw, seen)

6. We were glad to know Harvey had _____ back. (come, came, come)

7. At last night's party, most people _____ straight from work. (come, came, come)

8. The car has _____ too long without proper servicing (run, ran, run)

9. No matter how much he _____ before, I believe Pete has _____ himself this time. (do, did, done; outdo, outdid, outdone)

Answers: 1. gone 2. done 3. ran 4. run 5. saw 6. come 7. came 8. run 9. did; outdone

Little Words That Count a Lot

The following little adverbs never count as part of the verb itself. Yet they work closely with it and turn its meaning this way and that.

not	never	barely
hardly	scarcely	almost

- The program <u>has begun</u>.

  (S-V) [The] program/has begun

  The program <u>has</u> not <u>begun</u>.

  The program <u>has</u> barely <u>begun</u>.

  The program <u>has</u> only just <u>begun</u>.

  The program <u>has</u> almost <u>begun</u>.

- I <u>can understand</u> you.

  (S-V-C) I/can understand/you

  I <u>can</u> never <u>understand</u> you.

  I <u>can</u> hardly ever <u>understand</u> you.

  I <u>can</u> scarcely <u>understand</u> you.

  I <u>can't</u> <u>understand</u> you.

As an adverb, *not* can even attach itself by way of a contraction to the end of a verb, as in

can't	couldn't	shouldn't	wouldn't
mustn't	isn't	aren't	wasn't
weren't	don't	doesn't	didn't
hasn't	haven't	hadn't	won't

The shortened forms simply add *n't* (for *not*) to their regular form, except for *can't (can not)*, *won't (will not)* and—now rarely used—*shan't (shall not)*. Even attached, the *n't* isn't really part of the verb. It's still an adverb.

What's the difference?

- It <u>isn't</u> formal.

- It <u>is not</u> formal.

To be formal in speech or writing, avoid contractions. Writing out *not* makes the negative sense sound more emphatic, too.

- It <u>doesn't</u> seem right.

- It <u>does not</u> seem right.

Here are some other words that strike a negative note.

- I have <u>no</u> money.

- I saw <u>none</u> of my friends.

- You understand <u>nothing</u>.

- I met <u>nobody</u>.

ONE NEGATIVE IS ENOUGH

Using a double negative is one of the most noticeable errors you can make.

- (error) The Tigers didn't allow no base hits.
  (*n't* + *no* = a double negative)
  (correct) The Tigers didn't allow any base hits.
       The Tigers allowed no base hits.

- (error) I hadn't never seen a major league game before.
  (*n't* + *never* = a double negative)
  (correct) I had never seen a major league game before.
       I hadn't ever seen a major league game before.

It's usually easy to correct a double negative. Just get rid of one negative and keep the other one.

BE CAREFUL OF *OF*

- You would of liked the concert.

What's the *of* doing? Where does it come from? Maybe it's there because *of* sounds like *'ve,* a contraction for *have,* as in "You *should've* been there."

Should of, could of, ought to of, might of, would of—when you know how grammar works, you would have, ought to have, might have, must have, and definitely should have known that *of* is a preposition and can't be part of the main verb. The *of* should have been *have*.

- You would have liked the concert.
  (S-V-C) you/would have liked/[the] concert

Write a corrected version of each of the following sentences.

1. I didn't mean to insult nobody.

_____

2. It don't matter to me.

_____

3. Hank could have went back to work.

_____

4. If I was you, I wouldn't tell nobody what I done.

_____

5. The old dog would of laid there all day.

_____

6. There weren't nobody setting in the front row.

_____

7. The neighbors done all they could of to help.

_____

8. We never had no doubt that we seen a genius at work.

_____

9. When Monday come, we would of welcomed another weekend.

_____

Answers: 1. I didn't mean to insult anybody.—or—I meant to insult nobody. 2. It doesn't matter to me. 3. Hank could have gone back to work. 4. If I were you, I wouldn't tell anybody what I did.—or—I would tell nobody . . . 5. The old dog would have lain there all day. 6. There was nobody sitting in the front row.—or—There wasn't anybody . . . 7. The neighbors did all they could have to help. 8. We never had any doubt that we saw a genius at work.—or—We had no doubt that we saw a genius at work. 9. When Monday came, we would have welcomed another weekend.

INFINITIVES: TO SPLIT OR TO NOT SPLIT?

How do you split an infinitive? And who cares, anyway? Many grammar experts say it doesn't matter; some purists say it does. In Latin, an infinitive is only one word, which is impossible to split—and Latin grammar is the basis for the rule. Yet, as discussed in chapter 15, most English infinitives consist of two words: *to* + the base of the verb: *to go, to be, to come, to make, to know.* Here's how you might split an infinitive.

- <u>To</u> really <u>know</u> someone is difficult.

It seems to change the meaning to write, "<u>To know</u> someone really is difficult."

The best advice: When you have to genuinely work at splitting an infinitive—don't. If an unsplit infinitive seems to really destroy the balance of a sentence, go ahead and split it.

Did you spot the two split infinitives, *to work* and *to destroy,* in the previous two sentences? Are they necessary? Think how you would rephrase the sentences to avoid a split infinitive. Here are more examples.

- (split) It is time <u>to</u> actually <u>begin</u> working on the project, <u>to</u> not just <u>talk</u> about it.

- (unsplit) It is time actually <u>to begin</u> working on the project, not just <u>to talk</u> about it.

Putting Adverbs With Infinitives

According to the workings of word order, it's often possible to move an adverb around without greatly changing the meaning, as the following sentences show.

- The millionaire gives <u>generously</u> to worthy causes.

- The millionaire <u>generously</u> gives to worthy causes.

- The millionaire gives to worthy causes <u>generously</u>.

But what of the following? The infinitive makes moving an adverb trickier.

- I try <u>never</u> to be thoughtless.

- I <u>never</u> try to be thoughtless. (It just comes naturally?)

- I try to <u>never</u> be thoughtless. (Does splitting *to be* help?)

MAKING PERFECT USE OF PERFECT TENSES

The perfect tenses—present perfect, past perfect, and future perfect—give an idea of completion. Here are the rules for using them correctly.

1. The present perfect can be used alone and also works with present, past, future, or another present perfect tense.

    - You <u>have explained</u> the situation very well. (present perfect, alone)

    - I <u>am</u> sure that Al <u>has gone</u>. (present + present perfect)

    - Val's work <u>showed</u> that she <u>has studied</u> a great deal. (past + present perfect)

2. Combine the past perfect with a simple past to show that the first was completed before the second. The past perfect should not be used for both.

    - Jake already <u>had gone</u> when we <u>arrived</u>. (past perfect + simple past)

    - Kim <u>had known</u> about the meeting before I <u>told</u> her. (past perfect + simple past)

3. The future perfect speaks of a future event to take place before another future event.

    - I <u>will have forgotten</u> all my French by the time I <u>have</u> a chance to go to Paris. (future perfect + present)

    - Someone else <u>will have pointed</u> out the mistake before I <u>do</u>. (future perfect + present)

WATCH YOUR TENSES

In relating an incident, avoid switching back and forth in tenses. Choose the present or past, and stay with it unless there is dialogue or another good reason to change.

- (poor) Here I am, heading for my first experience at skiing. I was really nervous. I am not interested in making a fool of myself.

- (better) There I was, heading for my first experience at skiing. I was really nervous. I was not interested . . .

Identify the verbs in the following paragraph. Then write a revision, maintaining either present or past forms of the verbs, including perfect tenses if appropriate.

Greek mythology called Helen of Troy the most beautiful woman in Greece. She is the indirect cause of the Trojan War. She had been carried off from Sparta to Troy by Paris, who is the son of the Trojan king, at a time when her husband, Menelaus, was absent. Before she had married Menelaus, her father asks all her suitors to accept her choice, and they promised they will side with her husband if anyone would have done wrong to him in the future. When Menelaus discovers Helen was gone with Paris, the Greek men had kept their promise. They have attacked Troy. It is captured, and Helen returned home with Menelaus, with whom she remains happily as his wife as long as they lived.

_____

_____

_____

_____

_____

_____

_____

_____

_____

_____

Answer: Note: There is more than one correct way to rewrite this passage; here is one version.

The most beautiful woman in Greece according to Greek mythology, Helen of Troy was the indirect cause of the Trojan War. She had been carried off from Sparta to Troy by Paris, who was the son of the Trojan King, at a time when her husband, Menelaus, was absent. Before she married Menelaus, her father had asked all her suitors to accept her choice, and they promised they would side with her husband if anyone wronged him in the future. When Menelaus discovered Helen had gone with Paris, the Greek men kept their promise. They attacked and captured Troy. Helen returned home with Menelaus, with whom she remained happily as his wife as long as they lived.

SELF-TEST

For each sentence, choose the correct word of those in parentheses.

1. That statue looks as if it _____ really alive. (was, were)

2. The scrap of paper _____ on the walk was actually a blank check. (laying, lying)

3. It is better to _____ your goals too high than too low. (set, sit)

4. Have you ever _____ an eclipse of the sun? (see, saw, seen)

5. The cat loves to _____ on the window ledge. (set, sit)

6. How much good work you have _____ in restoring that old car! (do, did, done)

7. You _____ blame Carlos for being angry. (can hardly, can't hardly)

8. To pass the test, I _____ study hard. (had to really, really had to)

9. Chris had already heard the news before I _____ her about it. (told, had told)

10. Sydney hopes she will have gotten a good tan before she _____ for Baja California. (will have left, leaves)

11. No one could _____ better than you did. (of did, of done, have did, have done)

12. There _____ excuse for the rudeness of some drives. (isn't any, isn't no)

13. The dream of an explorer is to do what no one has ever _____ before. (do, did, done)

14. The time has _____ to prepare for the holiday. (came, come)

15. The boss insisted that the staff _____ on time. (be, was)

ANSWERS

1. were 2. lying 3. set 4. seen 5. sit 6. done 7. can hardly 8. really had to 9. told 10. leaves 11. have done 12. isn't any 13. done 14. come 15. be

20 Questions of Usage: How Can Words Agree When People Don't?

Which of the following is correct?

- Everyone has <u>his</u> own opinion.

- Everyone has <u>their</u> own opinion.

- Everyone has <u>his or her</u> own opinion.

One thing is sure. Almost everyone does have an opinion. An old-time schoolmaster would have had no problem drilling his pupils on the right answer. "Definitely," he would say, "it should be his." He had an excellent reason for being sure his version was right, and many of those on the lookout for mistakes in grammar would still agree. Among them is the *Associated Press Style Book,* accepted by many writers.

Does the choice you make really matter? It does to many.

"*His* opinion?" ask some. "What about *her*?" Their vote goes to the third example with *his or her,* just as they believe in replacing *salesman* with *salesperson* and *chairman* with *chairperson* to get rid of sexist overtones.

What about *their*? It may be the choice of someone who doesn't know grammar, or someone who avoids taking sides—or even be someone who doesn't know how to count!

In many ways, your choice of words involves more than how language works. It also expresses how you think and feel. For that reason, it's both what you say and how you say it that tell the whole story.

INDEFINITE PRONOUNS AND NOUNS

Everyone uses indefinite pronouns and nouns in everyday speech. In fact, an indefinite pronoun begins this paragraph. An **indefinite pronoun** doesn't refer to or name a specific person, place, or thing. Some don't even indicate a specific number, although they may be singular or plural. And, because of their indefinite nature, the rules for using them can seem confusing.

The Singular Indefinites

If you can remember one key indefinite pronoun, such as *everything*, the rest come easily. Then just take *every-, any-, no-,* and *some-* and pair them with *-one, -body,* and *-thing* in every way you can:

everyone	somebody	anything
no one	nobody	nothing
someone	everybody	something
anyone	anybody	everything

Others convey the same idea as those above:

each	either	neither
another	one	each one

Compare the following sentences:

- Chuck is coming.
- Lynn is coming.
- Everyone is coming.

Or, if the worst happens:

- No one is coming.

It's not hard to agree that each of these indefinite pronouns needs a singular verb, such as *is, was, has, does,* or *wants*.
   Now compare this set of sentences.

- Chuck has lost his jacket.
- Lynn has lost her jacket.
- Somebody has lost _____ jacket.

Here's where the trouble comes in today.

Those who hold with tradition would say, "Somebody has lost his jacket." Both *somebody* and *has* are singular. Obviously, the possessive adjective should agree.

"Sexist! It should be 'Somebody has lost his or her jacket,'" cries another.

"Too awkward," comes the reply. "Besides, *he* and *his* are pronouns that have traditionally been used indefinitely to mean either sex."

Who's right? In questions of grammar, logic doesn't necessarily win out. If you don't believe that, just look at that very illogical word *be,* the subject of chapter 13.

Some Indefinite Guidelines

- Everyone has their own opinion.
  Their is "wrong," even if it does solve the problem of sexism.

- Everyone has his own opinion.
  If you want your authority to be the old rule of grammar, backed by the AP, carry on the fight.

- Everyone has his or her own opinion.
  It is awkward, isn't it? And shouldn't it be "her or his"?

Whatever you choose, prepare to defend yourself, or try to avoid the situation by rephrasing the sentence.

- Everyone is entitled to an opinion.

- Someone has lost a jacket.

- You have your own opinion, just as everyone else has.

Indefinite Plurals: No Problem

Indefinite pronouns such as *everyone* and *each* single out one of a group and use it to stand for the rest. Four indefinite pronouns are strictly plural: *both, few, many,* and *several.* They always take plural verbs, possessives, and other pronouns in questions of agreement.

- Both of the plans have their good points.

- Few of the children's toys are ever as durable as they are advertised to be.

- <u>Several</u> of the guests have expressed their thanks.
- <u>Many</u> of the styles are still on sale.

Some Indefinite Pronouns Go Either Way

Certain indefinite pronouns can have either singular or plural senses, depending upon whether they deal with numbers or quantity.

- <u>Most</u> of the seats have been filled.
- <u>Most</u> of the room has been repainted.

The Most Indefinite of Indefinite Pronouns
(May Be Singular or Plural)

all	most
any	none
enough	plenty
more	some

How do you know whether their use in a sentence should be singular or plural? Just check to see what they refer to.

- Chocolate cake?
  Enough <u>is</u> left for dinner.
- Eggs?
  Enough <u>are</u> left for omelettes.
- An insult?
  All <u>is</u> forgiven.
- Debts?
  All <u>are</u> paid.

If the pronoun in question deals with a number of items that can be counted, use the plural. If it deals with a quantity, a combined unit, or a quality, use the singular.

- Some of the beads <u>were</u> difficult to pick up.
- Some of the sugar <u>has</u> spilled on the floor.

None also works either way, according to its intended effect.

- None of my suggestions <u>were</u> taken.

- None of us <u>is</u> ready to give the presentation.

Much, little, and *less* are used indefinitely only in matters of quantity or portion and so take singular verbs.

- <u>Less</u> was said about the problem than I expected.

- <u>Little</u> is known.

- <u>Much</u> is hoped.

What Is the Subject?

Many of the indefinite pronouns can also work as adjectives. The difference may be important in matters of agreement. Usage, or using words in a certain way, becomes a matter of habit. When there's doubt, knowing how a word works can help you make the right choice.

Compare the following sentences.

- <u>Each</u> of the cereal boxes is almost empty.
  (S-V-C) each/is/empty

- <u>Each</u> question deserves a thoughtful answer.
  (S-V-C) question/deserves/[a] answer

- <u>One</u> of the children has an identical twin.
  (S-V-C) one/has/[an] twin

- <u>Some</u> children are difficult to please.
  (S-V-C) children/are/difficult

Remember, it is the subject that controls the verb, not an adjective or an object of a preposition.

- Mary is the only one of my friends who is able to go.
  (S-V-C: Main Clause) Mary/is/one
    What one? <u>of my friends</u>
    What one? *who is able* modifies one
    (S-V-C: Adjective Clause) who/is/able
  Mary is one of my friends who are going.
  (S-V-C) Mary/is/one
    What one? <u>of my friends</u>
    What friends? *who are going* modifies friends

Note: *Who* is used as a relative pronoun in both sentences. Its verb depends upon its antecedent. In the first example, *who* replaces *one*; in the second it replace *friends*. Choose the verbs that match.
   Here is another point of agreement.

- There is plenty of time.
  (S-V) plenty/is

- There are plenty of potato chips.
  (S-V) plenty/are

There is often an introductory word, an expletive, or in some sentences, an adverb. It is not the subject.
   Always be sure to check for the true subject, whether or not *there* is used along with an indefinite pronoun.

DEMONSTRATIVE PRONOUNS AND ADJECTIVES

	Near	Not So Near
Singular	this	that
Plural	these	those

- <u>This</u> is my popcorn. <u>That</u> is hers.

- <u>These</u> are my pretzels. <u>Those</u> are yours.

- <u>This</u> Coke is mine. <u>That</u> Pepsi is yours.

- <u>These</u> tapes and CDs are my favorites.

   This and *these* carry a sense of being "here," while *that* and *those* imply being "there." For this reason, it's unnecessary and is even thought illiterate to include these adverbs in such sentences as:

- (wrong) This here is my bowl of popcorn, and that there is yours.
  (correct) This is my bowl of popcorn, and that is yours.

Don't use *them*, a pronoun, with *there* as a pointer. One word does the job.

- (wrong) I'd like one of them there candy bars.
  (correct) I'd like one of those candy bars, please.

Check the Subject-Verb of each sentence and clause. Then, from the pair in parentheses, select the word that agrees with the subject of the sentence or clause. Be careful—some subjects are relative pronouns.

1. Everybody in the cast _____ (is, are) ready for opening night but Neil.

2. Each of the cars _____ (has, have) good qualities of _____ (its, their) own.

3. Most of Voces Latinos' hits _____ (is, are) in Spanish.

4. _____ (Is, Are) any of the airlines offering special fares to Florida?

5. More paint _____ (is, are) needed to finish the job.

6. Most of the answers _____ (seems, seem) reasonable.

7. Fewer people _____ (has, have) made plans to come this year; less food _____ (is, are) needed.

8. Each of the novels that _____ (appears, appear) on the reading list _____ (was, were) written by a different author.

9. There _____ (is, are) a few members who do most of the work.

10. This _____ (is, are) one of the many problems that _____ (is, are) waiting for a solution.

Answers: 1. is 2. has; its 3. are 4. are 5. is 6. seem 7. have; is 8. appear; was 9. are 10. is; are

COMPOUND PERSONAL PRONOUNS

Person	Singular	Plural
1st	myself	ourselves
2nd	yourself	yourselves
3rd	herself, himself, itself	themselves

Use the compound form of a personal pronoun when its simple form or the noun it names is in the same sentence. There are three correct ways to use a compound personal pronoun.

1. Reflexive: when a person or thing acts upon itself

    • I asked <u>myself</u> what went wrong.
    • <u>He</u> cut <u>himself</u> on the sharp can lid.
    • Save a piece of cake for <u>yourself</u>. (*You* is the understood subject.)
    • <u>You</u> will do <u>yourselves</u> a favor by listening carefully.

2. Intensive: when repeated for emphasis

    • <u>They themselves</u> accept the full responsibility.
    • Only <u>she herself</u> can make that decision.
    • I know what <u>I myself</u> would do in that case.

3. When it acts as a predicate nominative.

    • <u>Mitzi</u> has not been <u>herself</u> recently.
    • After a rest, <u>he</u> became <u>himself</u> again.

Do not use the compound personal pronoun if it does not relate to another pronoun or noun in the same sentence.

• (ouch) You can expect cooperation from myself and my associates.
• (ouch) It is people like yourself who make this company successful.
• (ouch) My fiancee and myself wish to thank you.

Sentences like these are sometimes affected as examples of high-class grammar. They are simply wrong. It is better to say:

• (correct) You can expect cooperation from me and my associates.
• (correct) It is people like you who make this company successful.
• (correct) My fiancee and I wish to thank you.

Theirselves and *hisself* aren't accepted as compound personal pronouns . . . or even as respectable words.

- (ouch) People should take good care of theirselves by exercising and watching their diets.
  (correct) People should take good care of themselves by exercising and watching their diets.

- (ouch) Did you hear what he bought hisself?
  (correct) Did you hear what he bought himself?

AGREEMENT BETWEEN SUBJECTS AND VERBS

You've already met the general rule, introduced in chapter 3:

A verb agrees with its subject in person and number.

Most nouns form their plurals by adding *-s* or *-es*. The dictionary shows exceptions. A singular noun, singular indefinite pronoun, or third-person pronoun takes a present tense verb that ends in *s*. Note that a final *s* is usually the sign of plural for nouns, but the final *s* signals the singular present of verbs. It may seem backwards, but that's how it works.

- This photo <u>seems</u> out of focus.

- These photos <u>seem</u> out of focus.

With the majority of nouns and pronouns, making subjects and verbs agree is a matter of logic. First, you must be able to identify the subject, and that's where understanding grammar comes in.

In some cases, the correct choice is governed by usage, which is based upon custom. The questions of agreement discussed below include some of the most troublesome exceptions. Because customary usage deals with individual words, check a dictionary when you're in doubt.

Nouns That Look Plural But Act Singularly

Such nouns can be divided into three different categories.

1. Some nouns are commonly used with singular verbs although plural in form.

- news, politics, economics, athletics, molasses

- nouns that state a given time, weight, or amount of money

- titles of books, newspapers, television shows, even if plural form

Here are some examples.

- The <u>news</u> was watched by millions.

- <u>Athletics</u> is an important part of many people's lives.

- <u>Twenty dollars</u> goes fast.

- <u>Forty-five minutes</u> was all the time he could spare.

- *<u>The Times</u>* is known for its excellence.

- *<u>Star Wars</u>* has fans everywhere.

2. Some nouns are commonly plural in usage, even though naming something singular.

   - His <u>trousers</u> were old and torn.

   - <u>Scissors</u> are a great invention.

   - The <u>contents</u> were ruined.

   - The <u>suds</u> are almost down the drain.

   Others words used this way include *tweezers, clothes, wages,* and *oats.*

3. Collective nouns can be singular or plural. The decision depends upon the speaker or writer's intention. Most speakers of American English stay with the singular, although usage in Great Britain differs, with the plural more common. Collective nouns include such words as *family, public, audience, company, flock, team, bunch,* and *committee.*

   - The <u>committee</u> meets Thursday. (American)

   - The <u>committee</u> are having a lively discussion. (British)

   - When is the <u>family</u> moving? (American)

   - Herb's <u>family</u> are planning a surprise party for him. (British)

Many writers simply phrase sentences in another way to avoid using the plural verb with such collective nouns as these.

- The <u>committee</u> meeting is Thursday.
- A surprise party for Herb is being planned by his <u>family</u>.

How Compound Subjects Affect Agreement

Compound subjects joined by *and* are almost always plural.

- <u>Jed and Joyce</u> were arguing vociferously.
- <u>Cashews, olives, and avocados</u> are high in calories.
- <u>Danny and I</u> have never met.

The rare exceptions to this rule are based on the subject's being taken as a single unit.

- <u>Hide and seek</u> is a game I loved as a child.
- <u>My former roommate and still close friend</u> is Laura Radcliffe.

There are three possibilities for compound subjects joined with the conjunction *or*.

1. Because *or* gives a choice, singular words take a singular verb.

   - Steak or prime rib is today's choice of entree.

2. Plurals joined by *or* take a plural verb.

   - Are the Lakers or the Bulls ahead in the game?

3. If subjects differ, the verb agrees with the closer word.

   - Jan or her parents are likely to be home by now. (*Are* agrees with *parents*.)
   - Has Jane or her parents arrived home yet? (*Has* agrees with *Jane*.)

Some Subjects Look Plural But Aren't

- Jan, together with her parents, is planning Herb's party.
  (S-V-C) Jan/is planning/party
  How? together with her parents

Together with, as well as, in addition to, and similar expressions are not conjunctions and therefore do not form compound subjects. Watch for such phrases that are not really part of the subject, such as those in the following examples.

- Alice as well as Lydia is trying out for the role.

- The cost of repairs in addition to the purchase price puts the property beyond our reach.

Also, remember that the word *plus* is not a conjunction either, and so does not affect agreement.

- A cheeseburger plus fries and a milkshake is loaded with calories.

The Verb Agrees With Its Subject, Not Its Predicate Nominative
- Avocados are the main ingredient in guacamole.
  (S-V-C): Avocados/are/ingredient

BUT

- The main ingredient in guacamole is avocados.
  (S-V-C): ingredient/is/avocados

Identifying the True Subject
When introductory words are used in a sentence, always check to make sure of the actual subject.

- Where are the thumbtacks?
  (S-V) [the] thumbtacks/are

- Which of the twins is taller?
  (S-V-C) Which/is/taller

- Which model are you ordering?
  (S-V-C) you/are ordering/model

- There is someone tapping at the door.
  (S-V) someone/is tapping

- There are many unanswered questions.
  (S-V) questions/are

There, whether expletive or adverb, does not control the verb. *It,* whether expletive or pronoun, always takes a singular verb.

- It is sunny again today.

TIP

Two simple questions begin any analysis of how grammar works: Who or what is the sentence about? Who or what is doing something? They are also the key to solving tricky problems of agreement that depend on knowing which words actually power a sentence, no matter how complicated.

- It is my favorite show on television.

- It was a real surprise.

Select the correct form from the words in parentheses.

1. There is nothing else for Ron and _____ (me, myself) to do.

2. We will be delighted if both Beth and _____ (you, yourself) agree to serve on the committee.

3. The club officers kept their decision to _____ (them, themselves).

4. Good news _____ (is, are) less likely to arouse interest than bad news _____ (does, do)

5. Economics _____ (seems, seem) often to rely more upon opinions than facts.

6. The scissors in the kitchen _____ (is, are) not for use elsewhere.

7. Mel's wages _____ (is, are) higher than mine.

8. There _____ (is, are) no reason for you to feel rejected.

9. It _____ (is, are) people like you who are needed as volunteers.

10. Cookies and milk _____ (is, are) Kimmie's favorite dessert.

11. Either the heavy pounding of rain or the peals of thunder _____ (has, have) awakened me.

12. The early starting time, in addition to the low pay, _____ (is, are) not to my liking.

1. me 2. you 3. themselves 4. is; does 5. seems 6. are 7. are 8. is 9. is 10. is (if thought of as one unit) 11. have 12. is

21 Forming Comparisons Correctly: A Matter of Degree

Several of our hardest-working adjectives are irregular in the forms they use.

good	better	best
bad	worse	worst
many	more	most
much	more	most

With adjectives, the irregularity comes when making comparisons. In fact, in order to use grammar correctly, it's important to be aware of the exceptions and not to try to force them to fit the rule.

How often do we use comparisons? More often than you might guess.

- I like this color <u>better</u> than that.
- Jodie's camera was <u>more expensive</u> than mine.
- Steve is the <u>most dependable</u> person I know.

Comparisons are also found in countless advertising claims.

- Maxibrite gets teeth <u>cleaner</u> and <u>whiter</u>!
- You always get <u>more important</u> savings at ValuePlus!
- It's the store with the <u>BIGGEST</u> sales!

The question is not only "Are their claims true?" but also "Are the comparisons stated correctly?" As well as forming comparative forms correctly, you should become aware of the guidelines for using them, too.

TIP

Only descriptive adjectives have comparative forms.

First, recall the two types of work adjectives do in a sentence as they modify nouns and pronouns.
Adjectives can limit:

- This is <u>my</u> book.

- I know <u>that</u> woman.

- The Johnsons have <u>three</u> daughters.

Adjectives can also describe:

- That is a <u>good</u> book.

- I know that <u>young</u> woman.

- We heard the <u>surprising</u> news.

- That is a <u>good</u> book, but this is <u>better</u>.

THE DEGREES OF COMPARISON

The **positive** form of a descriptive adjective can be raised to the **comparative** and **superlative** degrees. The following examples illustrate the use of each.

Positive: Today was <u>warm</u>.

Comparative: Yesterday was <u>warmer</u>.

Superlative: It was the <u>warmest</u> July 5 on record.

Here are the basic rules for forming the comparative and superlative degrees.

1.   For most adjectives of one syllable and some of two syllables:

- Add an *-er* ending to the positive to form the comparative.

- Add an *-est* ending to the positive to form the superlative.

Positive	Comparative	Superlative
small	smaller	smallest
great	greater	greatest
calm	calmer	calmest

The positive form of some adjectives undergoes common spelling changes—sometimes the *y* becomes an *i* or a final letter doubles before the comparative ending, as in the examples below. Remember, dictionaries list such exceptions.

big	bigger	biggest
fat	fatter	fattest
lovely	lovelier	loveliest
pretty	prettier	prettiest

2. With adjectives of more than two syllables, and others that are hard to pronounce with an *-er* or *-est* ending:

    • Use the adverb <u>more</u> before the positive form for the comparative.
    • Use the adverb <u>most</u> as its indicator for the superlative.

Positive	Comparative	Superlative
important	more important	most important
curious	more curious	most curious
sensible	more sensible	most sensible
careful	more careful	most careful

3. Some adjectives work either way, depending upon the emphasis desired.

sad	sadder	saddest
	more sad	most sat
slim	slimmer	slimmest
	more slim	most slim
quiet	quieter	quietest
	more quiet	most quiet

4. A number of common adjectives are irregular:

good, well	better	best
little	littler -or-	littlest -or-
	less, lesser	least

late	later	latest
many, much	more	most
bad	worse	worst
old	elder	eldest
far	farther, further	farthest, furthest
northern	more northern	northernmost*

* as with other directions

In comparisons, adverbs follow the pattern of adjectives.

Positive	Comparative	Superlative
fast	faster	fastest
early	earlier	earliest
easily	more easily	most easily
carefully	more carefully	most carefully

TIPS FOR "PERFECT" USAGE

Some adjectives don't lend themselves to comparison. These include *complete, perfect, universal, unanimous,* and *faultless.*

- (correct) The crossword puzzle was <u>complete</u> and <u>perfect</u>.

How could you add anything more?

A word about *unique:* The main meaning of the word *unique* is "one of a kind."

- (questionable) That is a <u>most unique</u> piece of jewelry.

How can anything be most one of a kind? *Unique* becomes a weaker rather than a stronger word when you try to compare it, for then it simply means "quite unusual."

When you speak or write, try not to overuse strong comparative forms, but reserve such words as *best* for *the* best.

COMPARING THE COMPARATIVE AND SUPERLATIVE DEGREES

Use the comparative for comparing one thing to another.

- Joel is <u>taller</u> than his brother.

- I like butterscotch topping <u>better</u> than caramel.

- Jesse drives <u>more carefully</u> than Les.

- Which is the <u>shorter</u> of the two routes?

In using the comparative, make the comparison complete and clear.

- (unclear) An adult blue whale is larger than any mammal.
  Is a blue whale not a mammal? If it is, say "any other."
  (clear) An adult blue whale is larger than any other mammal.

- (unclear) Bev thinks she's smarter than anyone.
  Including herself? If not, add "else."
  (clear) Bev thinks she's smarter than anyone else.

- (unclear) Maxibrite gets teeth cleaner and whiter!
  Than what?
  (clear) Maxibrite gets teeth cleaner and whiter than any other brand of toothpaste.

   Oh, you know what I meant! Even so, it's best to assume words and sentences do mean what they say. Otherwise, there is nothing left to do but guess. One of the best reasons for knowing rules of grammar is that they provide people with an agreed-upon starting point for determining one another's meaning. Often it doesn't matter, but faulty phrasing can sometimes lead to serious misunderstandings.
   Here are more ways to be careful when making comparisons:

- (poor) A vacation in Mexico is less expensive than Europe.
  Comparing vacation to Europe?
  (better) A vacation in Mexico is less expensive than one in Europe.

- (poor) Which of the twins do you like best?
  How many are there? Use comparative for one-to-one comparisons.
  (better) Which of the twins do you like better?

Reserve the superlative for comparisons of more than two things.

- Kip is the most optimistic person I know.

- My most comfortable sweater is also my oldest one.

- Shakespeare's *Hamlet* is considered the greatest tragedy ever written in English.

With superlative comparisons, use *all*, not *any*.

- (poor) Marty thinks violets are the prettiest of any flower.
  (correct) Marty thinks violets are the prettiest flower of all.

SELF-TEST

Rewrite the following sentences to correct the confusing or incorrect comparisons.

1. Aunt Addie's angel food cake is always most perfect.

   _____

2. I like the BMW better than any car.

   _____

3. Which city is biggest, San Diego or San Francisco?

   _____

4. That is the most hard puzzle I ever tried to solve.

   _____

5. Dee comes to work earlier than anyone on the staff.

   _____

6. There is now more unanimous agreement on the need to protect the environment.

   _____

7. That computer is the most powerful of any.

   _____

8. Coming to work by bus is more economical than taxi.

   _____

9. What is the northernest state in the United States?

_____

10. My home is nearer to Lake Huron than any Great Lake.

_____

ANSWERS

1. Aunt Addie's angel food cake is always perfect. 2. I like the BMW better than any other car. 3. Which city is bigger, San Diego or San Francisco? 4. That is the hardest puzzle I ever tried to solve. 5. Dee comes to work earlier than anyone else on the staff. 6. There is now more nearly unanimous agreement on the need to protect the environment. 7. That computer is the most powerful of all. 8. Coming to work by bus is more economical than coming by taxi. 9. What is the northernmost state in the United States? 10. My home is nearer to Lake Huron than to any other Great Lake.

22 The Complete Sentence: Putting It All Together

What is a good sentence? One that works. By its classic definition, a sentence is a group of words that expresses a complete thought. True. Our system of grammar also shows that an English sentence is powered by a subject and a verb, usually in that order.

Then what about the three-word answer, "One that works," at the beginning of this chapter? Is it a sentence or just a piece or fragment of a sentence? Which is more effective as a direct answer to the question, "What is a good sentence?"

- One that works.

—or—

- A good sentence is one that works.

The second version, which correctly fits the textbook definition, dilutes the surprise. The first, by example, makes the point that the textbook definition has certain exceptions. It delivers its message in the fewest words possible and leaves you with something to think about. What more could you ask of a sentence?

ELLIPSIS: WHEN SOMETHING IS MISSING

The term *ellipsis* has two different senses in reference to grammar. Though they may seem very different at first glance, they share a common idea. Both refer to words left out of a sentence or paragraph.

1. As a form of punctuation, the ellipsis mark is a series of three dots (. . .) to indicate that words have been omitted, as discussed in chapter 11.

  - Dickens' statement, "It was the best of times, it was the worst of times . . ." describes almost any period of history.

2.   Ellipsis is also a term for the omission of words that are automatically understood and so don't need to be stated.

- A sentence expresses a complete thought.
  (S-V-C) sentence/expresses/[a] thought

- True.
  (S-V-C) That/is/true

Called **elliptical**, such sentences, clauses, and phrases come naturally in English, and they're readily understood. Ellipses are perfectly correct when they leave no doubt about what is meant and what is omitted. In fact, we object to sentences that repeat what we have every reason to know.

Ellipsis often accounts for the fact that some words in sentences don't seem to work in the regular way. In fact, often the omissions are not even noticed.

For example, ellipsis takes place with every use of a compound subject and verb, and also with imperatives.

- Pepe and Abbie just arrived.
  Pepe [just arrived] and Abbie just arrived.

- Hyland opened the door and walked in.
  Hyland opened the door and [Hyland] walked in.

- Come here.
  [You] come here.

Because English is a language of word order, the fluent speaker "hears" and automatically supplies what is missing.

Unfortunately, some students of grammar try to force all sentences to fit the definition rather allowing them to flow naturally. They write sentences that may be right according to the rules but are stiff and awkward.

Here are some more examples of ellipsis at work.

- He trusts her and she him.
- I will take the chance if you will, too.
- While in Puerto Rico, Whit became fluent in Spanish.
- My brother Vince is younger than I.

We don't "feel" anything missing, and it's easy to supply the understood words.

- He trusts her and she [trusts] him.

- I will take the chance if you will [take the chance], too.

- While [he was] in Puerto Rico, Whit became fluent in Spanish.

- My brother Vince is younger than I [am young].

Of course, if there is doubt, words must be supplied to make the idea complete and clear.

- I understand Glen better than you.

Better than I understand you?
Better than you understand Glen?

The revised versions may still be elliptical but are much clearer

- I understand Glen better than you do [understand Glen].

- I understand Glen better than I can [understand] you.

The purpose of a sentence is to deliver a thought, be it a statement, question, exclamation, or command. A good writer is not thinking of grammar when sitting down to write. There is an idea the writer needs to express. It's silly to imagine F. Scott Fitzgerald saying, "Let's see. I think I'll now write a compound-complex sentence with an introductory adverb clause and a couple of infinitive phrases." He had something more important on his mind, *The Great Gatsby.*

In spite of what is sometimes implied, an understanding of grammar is more important in reading and correcting errors than in helping a person write good sentences.

HOW SIMPLE OR COMPLEX?

A sentence should be no more complex than the thought it has to convey. Remember these guiding principles:

A complex thought can require a complex sentence.

A simple sentence fits a simple and direct idea best.

Sometimes people feel that dressing up a sentence improves it, as this anecdote shows. It is told by the physicist Richard P. Feynman in his memoir *Surely You're Joking, Mr. Feynman!*

There was a sociologist who had written a paper for us all to read—
something he had written ahead of time. I started to read the damn
thing, and my eyes were coming out: I couldn't make head or tail of it!
I figured it was because I hadn't read any of the books on that list. I
had this uneasy feeling of "I'm not adequate," until finally I said to
myself, "I'm gonna stop, and read one sentence slowly, so I can figure
out what the hell it means."

So I stopped—at random—and read the next sentence very carefully. I don't remember it precisely, but it was very close to this: "The
individual member of the social community often receives his information via visual, symbolic channels." I went back and forth over it, and
translated. You know what it means? "People read." Then I went over
the next sentence, and I realized that I could translate that one also.
Then it became a kind of empty business: "Sometimes people read;
sometimes people listen to the radio," and so on, but written in such
a fancy way that I couldn't understand it at first, and when I finally
deciphered it, there was nothing in it.

Sometimes complex sentences and difficult words are used merely to
impress others and make ordinary thoughts sound beyond the reach of
people who do not think of themselves as experts.

Also notice how Feynman, a Nobel Prize winner and one of the
world's greatest theoretical physicists, carefully and purposely avoids
seeming stuffy by using expressions such as "I'm gonna stop" and "what
the hell" when he writes.

Perhaps only an accepted genius or someone who really knows the
rules of grammar can get away with breaking them so freely!

TEN RULES FOR WRITING GOOD SENTENCES

Here are points to help you improve your writing and make it read more
smoothly and clearly.

1. Keep to the natural order unless you have a valid reason to change it.

    - (natural) The rabbit came out of the magician's hat.

    - (transposed) Out of the magician's hat came the rabbit.

    Transposing won't make a commonplace idea seem inspired.

2. Use the passive voice only when the subject or actor has little impor-
    tance.

- (active) Chains kept the prisoner from reaching the window.
- (passive) The prisoner was kept from reaching the window by the chains.

Sentences move faster in the active voice, but sometimes the idea comes across better in the passive.

3. Make sure that there is a clear reference to every pronoun.

- Ron told his boss that he didn't understand him.

Who doesn't understand whom? It does get tricky, but there is usually another way to phrase it without starting over.

- Ron accused his boss of misunderstanding him.
- Ron, not understanding his boss, asked him what he meant.

4. Don't allow an excessive number of words to get between a subject and its verbs.

- (poor) Early the next morning, the first thing Marcie did after turning off the alarm clock and putting on a robe and slippers was to go out on the balcony and look once again at the lovely view of the mountains.

$$\text{to go}$$
(S-V-C) thing/was/ [and]
$$\text{[to] look}$$

- (better) Early the next morning, after turning off the alarm clock and putting on her robe and slippers, Marcie went out on the balcony and looked once again at the lovely view of the mountains.

$$\text{went}$$
(S-V) Marcie/ [and]
$$\text{looked}$$

5. Use punctuation carefully. Don't create a fragment by using a period after a dependent clause or phrase that's too weak to stand alone.

- (incorrect) When it is wrongly set off as a sentence. A group of words is called a fragment.

- (correct) When it is wrongly set off as a sentence, a group of words is called a fragment.

Don't create a run-on by joining two sentences or dependent clauses with a comma. Punctuate them separately or use a conjunction or semicolon.

- (incorrect) A comma is not strong enough, it can't correctly join two sentences.

- (correct) A comma is not strong enough. It can't correctly join two sentences.

6. Avoid obvious repetition of a word, unless your purpose is to call attention to it.

- His face told me the news before he spoke. I could hardly face it. I turned my face to hide the sudden rush of emotion before turning to face him again.

A reader will get stuck in all the faces and hardly be able to make sense of the whole.

7. Be careful not to create confusion by putting words close together in a sentence if they have similar forms but different uses.

- Chet wanted to fish and to loaf, and to Tammy that was a boring kind of vacation.

The reader expects another infinitive instead of the prepositional phrase *to Tammy.*

- (better) Chet wanted to fish and to loaf, but Tammy thought that kind of vacation was boring.

- While I was waiting, watching the others sitting in the waiting room was very amusing.

Because of their different uses, the *-ings* in this sentence become confusing.

- (better) While I waited, I amused myself by watching the others with me in the waiting room.

8. Assume you will be taken literally. Don't leave out necessary words that will make your meaning clear.

- (poor) I have no need nor interest in your help.

- (better) I have no need for nor interest in your help.

- (poor) Checking the balance, a $200 error was found.

- (better) Checking the balance, I found a $200 error.

9. Make sure that a sentence really says what you mean it to say. Writing speaks for you, but it also must speak for itself. Try to leave no gaps, loopholes, or questions that the sentence itself (or those that follow) doesn't answer.

10. As a final step in writing, read your words as if you were a stranger to them. This is the time that your understanding of grammar is most helpful, when you check to be sure you've expressed yourself clearly.

A PARAGRAPH—MORE OR LESS—ABOUT PARAGRAPHS

A paragraph is a sentence or more of written or printed matter, dealing with a particular idea, printed as a unit, and usually indented at the beginning.

How do you know when to begin a new paragraph? It's actually the writer's choice. In practice, a paragraph can be as short as a single word as long as it contains a valid idea.

See?

How long can a paragraph be? Again, as long as the writer wishes. To create the effect he wished to achieve, author Rick Moody began his novel *Purple America* with a paragraph that continues for more than four pages.

SELF-TEST

There is generally more than one way to write a sentence. Compare each pair of sentences that follow. State whether A or B is correct and better written. Explain the reason for your choice.

1. a. Isak Dinesen is the pseudonym of Karen Blixen. Who was born in Denmark.

b. Karen Blixen, who used the pseudonym of Isak Dinesen, was born in Denmark.

2. a. Karen Blixen was a newlywed in 1914 when she and her husband, Baron Bror Blixen, arrived in Africa.
   b. First in 1914 arrived Karen Blixen in Africa, newly wed to her husband Baron Bror Blixen.

3. a. Dinesen is known for her memoir *Out of Africa* and is also known for short stories containing supernatural themes that have brought her renown throughout the world.
   b. Her memoir *Out of Africa* and her short stories containing supernatural themes have brought her renown throughout the world.

4. a. Dinesen wrote her first books in English and then rewrote them in Danish.
   b. Dinesen's books were initially written by her in English and then were rewritten in Danish.

5. a. The Blixens, who were cousins, divorced in 1921. Her love for Africa and its people led Dinesen, who was also a big-game hunter, to remain there 10 more years.
   b. The Blixens, who were cousins and big-game hunters, divorced in 1921, her love for Africa and its people led her to remain for 10 more years.

6. a. After living in Africa 17 years, the failure of her business drove her to sell her coffee plantation.
   b. After living in Africa 17 years, Dinesen sold her coffee plantation when her business failed.

Choice	Reason
1. _____	_____
2. _____	_____
3. _____	_____
4. _____	_____
5. _____	_____
6. _____	_____

ANSWERS

1. b, first version contains a fragment 2. a, transposed order causes confusion 3. b, version a contains repetitive use of known, renown 4. a, passive voice obscures meaning 5. a, other version is a run-on and contains a vague pronoun reference 6. b, version a lacks needed words

23 Making the Right Choices

"It ain't no crime to use 'ain't.'"

Some call it "murdering" English. Yet the rules of English usage aren't really laws. They are based on the system of grammar—the way words are organized in sentences to express their meaning most clearly and directly.

GOING BY THE RULES

When someone's grammar is incorrect it is usually because he or she made the wrong choice between two or more forms of what is basically the same word. The right choice is determined by the way a word is used in the sentence—how it works.

Possibly the most noticeable example is misusing *don't* for *doesn't*.

- (wrong) If it don't bother me, why should it bother anyone else? (But it does!)
  (correct) If it doesn't bother me . . .

It may not be fair, but those who know the right choices sometimes equate sloppy or careless use of language with sloppy thinking and carelessness in general. Although neither a sin nor a crime, breaking the rules of language may have negative consequences. In many situations and settings, your command of language is at least as important as how you look, dress, and behave.

Why Make Rules?

As writers like Robert Claiborne and Daniel J. Boorstein point out, the need for rules first became obvious with the invention of printing. They're arguably even more important today, when communication is done via the Internet between people great distances apart and impersonal communication speaks for you as a person.

In such situations as a face-to-face job interview, how you use language can say as much about you as the ideas you try to convey. Sometimes, it can even obscure your meaning.

How the Rules Change

A grammar book published in 1951 listed five different rules for people to follow when they used the words *shall* and *will*. The choice depended upon how the words worked in a sentence—whether they were expressing determination, "I will go," or simply politeness, "I shall be glad to go," for example.

Later in the same decade, another grammar book stated, "The distinction is . . . no longer important. They are used interchangeably." Today the difference is hardly worth mentioning.

The distinction has also blurred between "It's me" and "It's I." Should "It's me," once unacceptable, win out? Some still say no.

What's Next?

English is often called a universal language. It's true. English is learned in school by people all over the world because it's the language most likely to help you communicate wherever in the world you go, whether or not English is the native tongue.

In a bank in Athens, Greece, it should not seem strange to hear the teller conversing in English with a tourist from Japan. English is the one language they have in common.

Unfortunately, it sometimes seems that people who have learned English as a foreign language have a better grasp of its rules of grammar than many who claim it as their own.

It's true. People who know English can understand each other, even when it's spoken brokenly or sloppily. Yet knowing the rules and following them are important to those who want to communicate effectively to the greatest number of people and who want full attention paid to what they say, not how they say it.

Who's Kidding Whom?

In an effort to be friendly, catchy, and appealing to people who presumably don't know better, advertisers and copywriters frequently ignore the rules and show their indifference to the precise use of English.

- "Brand X has less calories."

- "Think different."

- "Cookies made good—just like you like 'em."

Calories must be counted. It should be ". . . has *fewer* calories," also, "Think differently" and ". . . made *well*—just *as* you like *them*."

According to a *Wall Street Journal* report, advertising agencies sometimes spend "weeks, even months, arguing whether to mangle the grammar in their copy—and how to mangle it and then justify their action when the calls . . . inevitably pour in."

For professional people like these, who know the rules, making the wrong choices is a way of talking down to people who don't know or aren't sure of those rules.

Where to Begin

When someone accuses another of using bad grammar, it's often a case of mixing together several different kinds of problems and treating them as if they were all the same.

The first problem area concerns choosing the right word when you speak, particularly words that change form depending upon how they work in a particular sentence. Major problems can arise when choosing:

among the three principal parts of verbs;

between subject and object forms of pronouns;

the verb form that agrees with the subject;

words that cause confusion because of usage or definition.

The second problem area involves writing. If the following sentence were spoken, there would be no problem: "Their is no doubt that there set in they're ways."

Because *their, there,* and *they're* are all pronounced almost the same way, our ears are trained to grasp the differences in meaning from the way they work, their place in the sentence, and the words used along with them—their context.

Major writing problems include:

spelling mistakes, especially of **homonyms,** words that sound alike but have different meanings;

incorrect punctuation and capitalization;

misuse of apostrophes in possessives and contractions;

confusing run-ons and fragments with correct sentences.

In setting out to improve your use of language, start by concentrating on the areas in which you have the most problems.

PROBLEM AREA 1: WHEN YOU SPEAK

Here are details of usage needing special attention when you speak.

1. Do be careful using *don't.*
   Does + not = doesn't (He doesn't; she doesn't; it doesn't. A person, place or thing doesn't.)

   • Does she, or doesn't she?

2. Know the difference between *he* and *him.*
   Also *I* and *me; she* and *her; we* and *us; they* and *them; who* and *whom.*

   • He is the subject of the news story; ask him what was said about him.

3. Don't be fooled by compound use of pronouns.

   • My friends and I have differing opinions about politics. (compound subject)

4. Put tricky forms of verbs in their proper places.
   Memorize the three principal parts of irregular verbs, such as *go* (go, went, gone).

   • Today I go; yesterday I went; I often have gone.

5. Make verbs and subjects agree: singular with singular; plural with plural.
   In present and present perfect tenses, singular verbs and helpers end in *-s.*

   • A bird flies. The season changes. A flower is growing. Rain has fallen. (singular)

- Birds fly. The seasons change. Flowers are growing. The rains have fallen. (plural)

6. Avoid asking an adjective to do the work of an adverb.
   Adverbs modify verbs, adjectives, and adverbs. Adjectives used properly don't.

   - That was a really generous offer; you really are a real friend.

7. Avoid asking an adverb to substitute for an adjective.
   After linking verbs such as *feel*, choose an adjective to modify the subject

   - I feel bad about your decision. The situation looks bad, so your help is badly needed.

8. Form and use comparative adjectives and adverbs correctly.
   Good, better, best; complex, more complex, most complex; quietly, more quietly, most quietly

   - I think this one is good. Which of the two do you like better? Which of the three do you like best?

9. Include necessary words to complete statements containing comparisons.

   - Jane thinks cats make the best pets of all. (not of any)

   - Olympic athletes train to be better than anyone else in their field. (not better than anyone)

10. Don't ask compound personal pronouns to work alone.
    Myself, himself, herself, itself, yourself, ourselves, yourselves, themselves—each of these needs a reference.

    - I sometimes talk to myself.

    - The President himself made that decision.

11. Limit yourself to one negative per clause; do not use double negatives.
    Such pairings as *doesn't hardly, hasn't no, almost couldn't* sound illiterate.

- It doesn't seem right.—or—It hardly seems right.

- He hasn't any sense.—or—He has no sense.

12. Match verbs carefully when sentences have compound subjects.
    Compound subjects joined by *and* are usually plural; the word nearer the verb controls those joined by *or*.

    - A month or four weeks are nearly the same.

    - Four weeks and a month is nearly the same.

    - A month and four weeks are too long to wait.

1. In each of the following sentences, choose the word in parentheses that works correctly in the sentence.

    a. The changing seasons _____ (is, are) what some people miss most in Florida.

    b. Torrid weather _____ (don't, doesn't) seem to bother other people.

    c. There is _____ (hardly any, hardly no) subject more popular than the weather for opening a conversation.

    d. Either the weather or the latest crime news _____ (is, are) usually talked about first.

    e. It is _____ (sure, surely) difficult for a born-and-bred Floridian to imagine someone preferring months of snow.

    f. To many Michiganders winter is the best season _____ (of all, of any).

    g. Just between you and _____ (I, me, myself), I find their attitude quite extreme.

    h. Summer weather is perfect for _____ (I, me, myself).

    i. Those who love winter feel _____ (bad, badly) about unseasonably high temperatures.

    j. For winter sports enthusiasts, the weather forecast is the _____ (importantest, most important) part of a newscast.

k. In discussions, fans of any seasons have often _____ (take, took, taken) a position that angered partisans of another.

l. Anyone _____ (who, whom) you ask almost surely has an opinion about the weather.

Answers: a. are b. doesn't c. hardly any d. is e. surely f. of all g. me h. me i. bad j. most important k. taken l. whom

2. The following sentences contain multiple errors in the choice of words. Identify these mistakes, and write a corrected version of each sentence.

a. Otis don't have no idea why he done so poor on the entrance exam.

_____

b. Margie says she feels real bad that you and him don't agree on which one is the best of the two plans.

_____

_____

c. Anyone who you ask will tell you that Mr. Hendricks and them haven't spoke to each other for years.

_____

_____

d. Max and yourself should join my husband and I for this real special exhibit at the Museum of Modern Art.

_____

_____

e. Although Sally and her is twins, Sissy is the tallest one.

_____

f. It don't hardly seem fair that they give Ken the reward when Stan seen the lost billfold first.

_____

_____

g. People who think they're more smart than anybody often believe nobody can never fool them and wind up fooling theirselves.

_____

_____

h. Either Jan or myself are pretty sure to find time to help you and he.

_____

i. Do you think that her or Joyce is the best choice, or is Grant better than anyone to chair the group?

_____

_____

j. What he done isn't nobody's business, but his action has showed he thinks he's beter than you or I.

_____

_____

Answers: a. Otis doesn't have any idea why he did so poorly on the entrance exam.

b. Margie says she feels really bad that you and he don't agree about which is the better of the two plans.

c. Anyone whom you ask will tell you that they and Mr. Hendricks haven't spoken to each other for years.

d. You and Max should join my husband and me for this really special exhibit at the Museum of Modern Art.

e. Although Sally and she are twins, Sissy is the taller one.

f. It doesn't seem (*or* hardly seems) fair that they gave Ken the reward when Stan saw the lost billfold first.

g. People who think they're smarter than everybody else often believe nobody can ever fool them and wind up fooling themselves.

h. Either Jan or I are quite sure to find time to help you and him.

i. Do you think that she or Joyce is the better choice to chair the group, or is Grant best to chair the group?

j. What he did isn't anybody else's business, but his actions have shown that he thinks he's better than you or me. — *or* — What he has done is nobody else's business, but his actions showed that he thinks he's better than you or me.

Saying What You Mean

A word may sound close to one that's right, yet not hold exactly the sense it is asked to express by an incautious speaker. Even a thesaurus may list synonyms that are correct in one sense of a word but not in another.

For example, the reviewer of a newly released recording wrote, "When this album glows, it really glowers."

Glow, glower, glowest. The review sounds really glowing, doesn't it? The problem is that *glower* has nothing to do with *glow,* for *glower* means "to scowl or stare with bad humor or anger."

Being precise in what you say or write does matter. Try not to use an unfamiliar word or one you're not sure of. In some cases, misuse has caused the differences to blur, but it is well to observe the distinctions. When in doubt, use the dictionary.

Words and Phrases Easily Confused

amount, number

amount: (n.) refers to a quantity considered a unit; use singularly.

- The amount of confusion here is incredible.

number: (n.) refers to items that can be counted; use with plurals except when referring to a number as a whole.

- A number of Canadian geese were sighted. (plural)

- The number of people owning computers is enormous (singular)

anxious, eager

anxious: (adj.) means "worried, uneasy."

- The test made Terry anxious.

eager: (adj.) means "looking forward to, wanting very much."

- The children were eager for the vacation to begin.

bad, badly

bad: (adj.) means "not good, not as it should be."

- The casserole tasted bad to me.

badly: (adv.) means "in a bad manner."

- The suit fit badly.

beside, besides
    beside: (prep.) means "by the side of."

- The house was built beside the lake.

    besides: (prep., adv.) in addition to

- No one is home besides us.

between, among
    between: (prep.) use with regard to two things.

- Choose between the gold and silver frames.

    among: (prep.) used with more than two things.

- Among her treasures are several rare shells.

continue on, refer back, cancel out
    Continue means "to go on," so adding *on* after *continue* is not needed. Similarly, the definitions of *refer* and *cancel* make *back* and *out* repetitious.

- Continue what you are doing. Refer to the table of contents. Cancel the reservation.

could care less
    This phrase means you do care a little. If you don't care at all, say: "I *couldn't* care less."

could of, would of, should of
    Do not use the preposition *of* in place of the helping verb *have*.

- He should have known better. Most people would have acted differently.

done, did
    done: used as a verb, needs a helper.

- Few have done such a deed.

    did: the simple past of do.

- He did that, didn't he?

doesn't, don't
    doesn't: use with singular pronouns (except *I* and *you*) or nouns.

- It doesn't do to forget this.

don't: use with plural pronouns and nouns, and with *I* and *you.*

- These gloves don't match.

etc.

 etc.: an abbreviation of *et cetera,* meaning "and so forth." Do not add unneeded words.

- (poor) There will be hot dogs, chips, coleslaw, and etc.
(poor) There will be picnic food such as hot dogs, chips, coleslaw, etc.
(better) There will be hot dogs, chips, coleslaw, and other picnic favorites.

fewer, less

 fewer: (pron., adj.) use only with items that are plural.

- Fewer changes than we expected were made.

 less: (pron., adj.) use only in matters of a coherent unit, quantity, or portion.

- People seem to have less free time (*or* fewer leisure hours than in the past).

from, off

 from: (prep.) use *from,* not *off,* with persons.

- I borrowed the notes from Arnie.

 off: (prep.) when used in the sense of from, do not add of.

- Get that cat off the table.

good, well

 good: (adj.) means "having wanted qualities."

- That was a good try.

 well: (adj.) means "healthy, comfortable."

- A well person usually has a good skin color.

 well: (adv.) is the adverbial form of good.

- She does well in school.

hardly, scarcely

Both words are negative; don't use another negative form with either one.

- (incorrect) It doesn't hardly matter to me.
  (right) It hardly matters to me.

healthy, healthful

healthy: (adj.) means "having or resulting from good health."

- Magazines feature many articles on how to be healthy.

  healthful: (adj.) means "helping to produce health, wholesome."

- Healthful foods help you remain healthy.

if, whether

if: (conj.) expresses possibility, meaning "in the case that."

- If the opportunity arises, seize it.

  whether: (conj.) expresses doubt; may be used with *or not*.

- No one can be sure whether the rumor is true.

in, into, in to

in: (prep.) indicates a position within.

- The letter is in the mail.

  into: (prep.) indicates movement from without to within.

- She reached into the refrigerator.

  in to: two words doing different work in the sentence.

- He came in to see what was causing such an uproar.

  (*In* is an adverb, *to,* the sign of the infinitive *to see.*)

kind of, sort of

Both, which are used interchangeably, should be used as a noun plus preposition, not in the sense of an adverb meaning *rather.*

- (poor) What kind of a book do you like best?
  (correct) What kind of book do you like best? (Leave out the *a.*)

- (poor) I sort of like science fiction.
  (correct) I rather like science fiction.

leave, let

leave: (v.) means "to go away or depart."

- The flight leaves at 8 a.m.

let: (v.) means "to permit or allow."

- My schedule won't let me attend.

- (incorrect) Leave me watch this show for a minute.
(correct) Let me watch it.

like, as, as if

like: (prep.) Often used in everyday speech as a conjunction; formerly considered proper only when used as a preposition.

- (prep.) That looks like fun.

as, as if: (conj.) means "to the same degree, in manner that"

- (questionable) That looks like it would be fun.
(correct) That looks as if it would be fun.

most, almost

most: (n., adj.) means "the greatest amount."

- Most of the answers were clear.

almost: (adv.) means "very nearly, all but."

- It's almost time to leave.
- (incorrect) Most all of the answers were clear.
(correct) Almost all of the answers were clear.

plan on coming

plan: (v.) When used as a verb, *plan* should be followed by an infinitive, not by a prepositional phrase.

- Plan to come.

raise, rise

raise: (v.t.) means "to lift, to cause to go up."

- They raise the flag each morning.

rise: (v.i.) means "to ascend, to move up to a higher level."

- Our hope is rising.

reason is because

reason: (n.) Since *reason* means "a cause or explanation," adding *because* is repetitious.

- (repetitive) The reason he made the mistake was because of his carelessness.
  (correct) The reason he made the mistake was his carelessness.
  (correct) He made the mistake because of his carelessness.
  (correct) He made the mistake because he was careless.

them, those

them: (pron.) is not properly used as an adjective.
those: (adj., pron.) used to point out something specific.

- (incorrect) Them neighbors of ours are real friendly.
  (correct) Those neighbors of our are really friendly.

these kind, those sort

Since both *kind* and *sort* are singular; use *this* or *that* to modify them.

- Do you prefer this sort of cooking or do you like that kind better?

try and come

The intended meaning is usually not "try and then come," but "try to come."

- (misused) Try and come to the party.
  (correct) Try to come to the party.

where

Where means "to, in, or at what place." Do not use it in place of *that*.

- (wrong) I hear where you've been promoted.
  (correct) I hear that you've been promoted.

Because *at* and *to* are within the meaning of *where,* don't add either after it.

- (wrong) Where is it at? Where are you going to?
  (correct) Where is it? Where are you going?

would have, could have

Use *had* as the helping verb instead of *would have* in clauses beginning with *if* and expressing doubt.

- (faulty) If you would not have come, there could have been a problem.
  (correct) If you had not come, there could have been a problem.

Make the correct choice from the words in parentheses.

1. There might have been more we _____ (could have, could of) done if we _____ (had, would have) known earlier.

2. _____ (Almost all, most all) of the staff members are at their desks early.

3. Tory was _____ (anxious, eager) to get the job but _____ (anxious, eager) about the interview.

4. No one should feel _____ (bad, badly) about the loss because everyone _____ (did, done) all that was possible to help.

5. The management plans _____ (on moving, to move) ahead with construction of its new headquarters.

6. _____ (A, An) minute can seem like _____ (a, an) hour when you are in _____ (a, an) hurry.

7. I got the news _____ (from, off, off of) Peter that hardly _____ (anybody, nobody) has made reservations so far.

8. Most people seem to feel they'd have _____ (fewer, less) problems if they only _____ (had, would have) more money.

9. Having money may simply change the kind, not the _____ (amount, number) of problems you have.

10. As the temperatures _____ (raise, rise), it becomes harder to try _____ (and, to) keep your mind _____ (off, off of) your vacation.

11. _____ (If, Whether) everyone likes the conclusion or not, it looks _____ (as if, like) the negotiators have reached a decision.

12. Some people act as if they _____ (could, couldn't) care less about eating _____ (healthful, healthy) and nutritious food.

13. Food, coats, gloves, blankets _____ (and etc., etc., and so on,) are needed by victims of the disaster.

14. If it's true there is honor _____ (among, between) most thieves, it _____ (doesn't, don't) seem true of those I know about.

15. Has anyone _____ (beside, besides) me noticed _____ (a kind of, kind of a) secretive look on Emme's face?

16. As he walked _____ (in, into, in to) the darkened room, Will was aware of a strange silence _____ (in, into, in to) the house.

17. The reason was _____ (because, that) all of his friends were hiding, waiting to rush _____ (in, into, in to) cry, "surprise!"

18. Although Will _____ (doesn't, don't) like _____ (that, those) sort of surprise, he knew his friends meant _____ (good, well) and tried to look pleased.

19. When you agree to _____ (leave, let) some telephone sales-people have a minute of your time, you do _____ (good, well) to get rid of them without being rude.

20. Did you hear _____ (that, where) Fly-by-Nite airlines has one of _____ (them, those) bargain packages to Florida that only _____ (continues, continues on) another week?

Answers: 1. could have; had 2. Almost all 3. eager; anxious 4. bad; did 5. to move 6. A; an; a 7. from; anybody 8. fewer; had 9. number 10. rise; to; off 11. Whether; as if 12. couldn't; healthful 13. etc. 14. among; doesn't 15. besides; a kind of 16. into; in 17. that; in to 18. doesn't; that; well 19. let; well 20. that; those; continues

PROBLEM AREA 2: WHEN YOU WRITE

No one becomes confused about *their, there,* and *they're* when someone is speaking. That's because it's easy to understand their meanings when they are heard in context in conversation.

Confusion does arise when people read, for they tend to associate a word's spelling with actual meaning, not with its context. "When people rite, its sometimes hard to tell they're meaning."

Three words in the previous sentence don't actually mean what they are supposed to mean. *Its* means "belonging to it," not "it is." *They're* means "they are," not "belonging to them." A *rite* is a ceremony. To read clearly, the sentence should be written: "When people write, it's sometimes hard to tell their meaning."

When words on paper or on a screen are all you have to represent yourself, it's even more important to be careful in your use of language. In Problem Area 2, choosing the right word is still important, but there are other details to watch when you put your words in writing.

All . . . That's Fit to Print

Lewis and Clark were explorers, not writers. Yet they both kept journals of their expedition of 1803 to 1806 to explore the land America acquired through the Louisiana Purchase and the territory beyond to the Pacific Ocean.

Should spelling and similar details matter to two explorers with genuine dangers to face? Hardly, but this excerpt from William Lewis's journal shows how such details do matter to readers. This passage from Lewis's journal seems difficult to read because of its incorrect word choices, spelling, capitalization, and punctuation. Identify the details that differ from the accepted usage of today, and write a corrected version.

> 21st December Friday 1804
> the Indian whome I stoped from Commiting Murder on his wife, 'thro jellosy of one of our interpeters, Came & brought his two wives and Shewed great anxiety to make up with the man with whome his joulussey Spring. a Woman brought a Child with an absess, . . . and offered as much Corn as she Could Carry for some Medison.
>
> [William Lewis]

_____

_____

_____

_____

Getting It Right in Writing

Here are some points you should keep in mind when you write.

1. Take responsibility for your spelling.

    When in doubt, check, but don't completely trust a computer spell-check. To it, there's nothing wrong with writing "I bought a hook," instead of "a book."

2. Pay particular attention to homonyms.

    The correct choice between words that sound alike but are spelled differently—from beau/bow to wright/write—is essential when you write.

3. Write complete, correct sentences.

    Words combined into sentences are the basic unit of written communication. A capital letter begins and a strong punctuation mark—period, question mark, or exclamation point—ends them.

4. Beware of unintentional fragments. Like this one.

    It's incorrect to punctuate clauses or phrases—like this one—as if they were sentences. Check before or after for an independent clause that completes the thought.

5. Watch for run-ons; they ask too much of a comma.

    Two independent clauses, which could stand alone as sentences, need something stronger—a semicolon or conjunction—to be correct.

6. Know how the apostrophe (') is used to punctuate words written as contractions.

    Use apostrophes to indicate shortened forms of verb + *not,* such as *doesn't, weren't, shouldn't,* and pronoun + verb, such as *I'm, you're, he's, they've, he'd, we'll.*

7. Know what words require apostrophes to signal possession.

    To show possession, a noun needs an apostrophe before *s* (*'s*) if singular, after *s* (*s'*) if it has a regular plural: Kiki's key; animals' habitats. Irregular plurals take *'s*: women's shoes. Possessive pronouns have no apostrophes: her key, their habitats, its design.

8. Remember, confusing *it's* and *its* is an error in spelling, not speaking.

    Along with *there's* and *theirs,* plus many others, these words sound alike when you speak. When writing, think of meaning: *it's* means "it is": *there's* means "there is."

9. Let a pair of commas set off nonessential phrases and clauses.
    Put commas at the beginning and end of embedded elements not necessary to a sentence.

    - Mr. Braun, whom I'd like you to meet, is my boss.
      Use a single comma if such words come at the beginning or end.

    - I'd like you to meet Mr. Braum, who is my boss.

10. Put commas around added, explanatory words contained in a sentence.
    Such additions as the date following day, state following city, and similar identification should be set off.

    - Their daughter, Casey, was born on Feb. 14, Valentine's Day.

11. Check the dictionary for spellings of irregular plurals and verbs.
    A computer spell-check offers multiple choices instead of providing you with the correct spelling of irregular forms as a dictionary does.

12. Be sparing with your use of fancy and powerful punctuation marks.
    Put quotation marks around direct quotations, with commas or periods inside. Avoid using "quotes" for "effect" . . . exclamation marks, too!!!

Correct errors in punctuation, capitalization, and spelling in the following sentences. Use quotation marks around quoted definitions, and underline titles of books.

1. *malapropism* is a word derived from the name of mrs malaprop a charcter in a play by richard sheridan

    _____

2. mrs. malaprop liked to use fancy unusual and high-sounding words but she used them in the wrong place

    _____

3. a newspaper columnist who was writing about media excesses said when all these forces gloom on to a story its not a pretty sight

_____

4. since he couldnt have meant that the forces became gloomy or sad which is the definition of gloom

_____

5. the writer should have use _glom_ which means to grab hold of he is guilty of a malapropism

_____

6. theres also the possibility that the error in a toledo ohio newspaper could have been a compositors misteak

_____

7. besides mrs malaprop do you know of other names from literature that are comonly used in english

_____

8. shangri-la was a mythical kingdom in james hiltons novel lost horizon it now means a paradise on earth

_____

9. because dickens creation ebenezer scrooge was a miser a inhumane boss and an miserable man who hates christmas

_____

10. would you be surprised to learn the saxophone was invented by a j sax a belgian who also invented the saxhorn

_____

Answers: 1. _Malapropism_ is a word derived from the name of Mrs. Malaprop, a character in a play by Richard Sheridan. 2. Mrs. Malaprop liked to use fancy, unusual, and high-sounding words, but she used them in the wrong places. 3. A newspaper columnist, who was writing about media excesses, said, "When all these forces gloom on to a story, it's not a pretty sight." (*You may omit the commas around "who was . . . excess" if you consider it essential.*) 4. He couldn't have meant that the forces "became gloomy or sad," which is the definition of *gloom.* 5. The writer should have used *glom,* which means "to grab hold of," and so he is guilty of a malapropism. (*The run-on may be corrected in other ways.*) 6. There's also the possibility that the error in a Toledo, Ohio, newspaper could have been a compositor's mistake. 7. Besides *malapropism,* do you know of other words from literary sources or people's names that are commonly used in English? 8. Shangri-la, which now means a practice on earth, was a mythical kingdom in James Hilton's novel *Lost Horizon.* (*The run-on may be corrected in other ways.*) 9. Dickens' creation, Ebenezer Scrooge, was a miser, an inhumane boss, and a miserable man who hated Christmas. (*The fragment may be corrected another way.*) 10. Would you be surprised to learn the saxophone was invented by A. J. Sax, a Belgian, who also invented the saxhorn?

Words That Spell Trouble

Certain words need to be chosen carefully, whether you are speaking or writing. Others require extra caution when you write.

Are they correctly spelled as one word or two? Can they be used either way, depending upon their meaning? Do they sound alike, or so nearly alike that it's hard to know which to use when?

Here is a list of words that frequently trip up someone who is careless or unwary. Correct use of such words helps identify a person who knows the English language and has mastered its use.

Look-Alike Words That Trap the Unwary

accept, except

accept: (v.) to receive, to agree to (I *accept* your generous offer.)

except: (prep.) but; (v.) to leave out, exclude (Everyone *except* Arthur has paid the fee.)

advice, advise

advice: (n.) opinion, suggestions about what to do (He never follows anyone's *advice.*)

advise: (v.) to give recommendations (The expert *advises* people about investing.)

affect, effect

affect: (v.) to influence, stir emotions (The storm *affected* a large area.)

effect: (n.) result; (v.) to bring about (What *effect* did the change have on your plans?)

a lot, alot, allot

a lot: a great deal; *a lot* should always be two words (There have been *a lot* of questions about the new ruling.)

allot: (v.) to distribute in specific shares (Each state is *allotted* two senators.)

already, all ready

already: (adv.) previously (I have *already* spent more than I should have.)

all ready: completely prepared (Everything is *all ready* for the surprise party.)

Other words such as *almost/all most* and *altogether/all together* also have two correct versions, according to meaning. *All right* is the only acceptable choice, never *alright*.

anyway, any way

anyway: (adv.) in any case, at any rate (In spite of the warning, he did it *anyway*.)

any way: one of all possible methods (Is there *any way* to please you?)

awhile, a while

awhile: (adv.) for a short time (Stay *awhile*.)

a while: (n.) a period of time (It took quite *a while* to finish the job.)

beside, besides

beside: (prep.) at the side of (The child sat *beside* his father.)

besides: (adv., prep.) in addition to (There are problems *besides* those which you know about already.)

capital, capitol, Capitol

capital: (n.) an uppercase letter; a city that is the seat of a state or national government; money or property owned or used in business (The *capital* of New York is Albany.)

capitol: (n.) the building in which a state legislature meets (The state senate meets in the *capitol*.)

Capitol: (n.) the building in which the U.S. Congress meets (The *Capitol* is in Washington, D.C.)

complement, compliment

complement: (n.) that which completes or perfects (That sweater is the perfect *complement* to your suit.)

compliment: (n.) words said in praise; an act of courtesy (It is sometimes hard to accept a *compliment* gracefully.)

conscience, conscious

conscience: (n.) an awareness of right and wrong (A troubled *conscience* may make it difficult to sleep.)

conscious: (adj.) awake; able to think and feel (I was *conscious* of voices talking in the other room.)

desert, dessert

desert: (n.) a dry, sandy, uninhabited region; deserved reward or punishment (The *desert* is inhospitable to many forms of life.)

dessert: (n.) the final course of a meal, typically something sweet (No, you can't eat your *dessert* first.)

dual, duel

dual: (adj.) double, of two (The response had a *dual* purpose.)

duel: (n.) a prearranged fight between two people with a chosen weapon (The challenge to a *duel* resulted from an exchange of insults.)

envelop, envelope

envelop: (v.) to wrap up; to surround; to conceal, hide (Fogs often *envelop* this stretch of the road.)

envelope: (n.) a folded paper container for letters, etc. (The *envelope* was torn, but the letter was untouched.)

explicit, implicit

explicit: (adj.) clearly stated or shown (The directions were *explicit* so everyone knew exactly what to do.)

implicit: (adj.) suggested but not directly expressed; implied (There was an *implicit* threat in his words and manner.)

farther, further

farther: (adj., adv.) more distant; at an actually greater distance (How much *farther* do we have to travel?)

further (adj., adv.) additional; to a greater degree or extent (How much *further* are you to continue this argument?)

faze, phase

faze: (v.) to disturb, bother (No amount of noise or commotion seems to *faze* some people.)

phase: (n.) any stage in a series; an aspect or side (Adolescence is often a troublesome *phase* of life.)

holy, holey, wholly

holy: (adj.) sacred (Sightseers should show respect at *holy* sites.)

holey: (adj.) full of holes (Why do you keep that *holey* old sweater?)

wholly: (adv.) entirely (I don't *wholly* agree with that theory.)

imply, infer

imply: (v.) to put in an idea or suggestion, not openly stated (The manager *implied* that he knew what the next move would be.)

infer: (v.) to draw a conclusion about something not openly stated (I *inferred* she knew what the next step would be.)

Noun forms: *implication* and *inference*

loose, lose, loss

loose: (adj.) free, unconfined; (v.) to set free or make less tight (The dog wriggled out of the *loose* collar.)

lose: (v.) to fail to win, get, etc.; to become unable to find (Our team was not expected to *lose* the game.)

loss: (n.) something lost (The *loss* of the game was unexpected.)

medal, metal

medal: (n.) a badge of inscribed metal, in memory of something special (An Olympic gold *medal* is the ultimate honor for a skater.)

metal: (n.) a mineral or ore, such as iron or gold (An alloy is a mixture of *metals*.)

meddle, mettle

meddle: (v.) to interfere (Gossips love to *meddle* in other people's business.)

mettle: (n.) courage, spirit (Disasters force people to show their *mettle* or their lack of it.)

parameter, perimeter

parameter: (n.) a quantity with assigned constant values (The *parameters* of the project were set to insure its success.)

perimeter: (n.) the outer boundary (The *perimeter* of the yard is outlined with a hedge.)

personal, personnel

personal: (adj.) private, individual (*Personal* preferences determine people's choices.)

personnel: (n.) the staff employed in any business, enterprise, etc. (A company's *personnel* always reflects its management's attitude towards doing business.)

precede, proceed

precede: (v.) to come or go before in time, place, rank, etc. (Introductory announcements *preceded* the dinner.)

proceed: (v.) to carry on, especially after stopping (After a few moments, the discussion *proceeded* as vigorously as before.)

preposition, proposition

preposition: (n.) a part of speech showing the relationship between words (Some people object to a *preposition* coming at the end of a sentence.)

proposition: (n.) something put for consideration, a plan (If a *proposition* sounds too good to be true, consider it carefully.)

principal, principle

principal: (adj.) leading, chief; (n.) head of a school; amount of a debt or investment, minus interest (The *principal* is the *principal* administrator in a school.)

principle: (n.) a fundamental truth; guiding rule (A person who has *principles* uses them as a basis for making decisions.)

prophecy, prophesy

prophecy: (n.) a prediction of the future (No one was surprised when the madman's *prophecy* didn't come true.)

prophesy: (v.) to make a prediction (Fortune tellers often *prophesy* something their customers want to hear.)

receipt, recipe

receipt: (n.) a written acknowledgement of something received; a welcome, receiving, or being received (Even if you have lost the *receipt*, the store will let you return the purchase.)

recipe: (n.) a list of materials and directions for preparing something; a formula (Octogenarians are sometimes asked their *recipe* for a long life.)

stationary, stationery

stationary: (adj.) not moving or not movable; still; unchanging (The *stationary* fixtures are all custom made.)

stationery: (n.) writing materials, especially paper and envelopes (Business *stationery* usually has a distinctive letterhead.)

than, then

than: (conj.) used to introduce the second element in a comparison (Does anyone have more fun *than* we do?)

then: (adv.) at that time; besides, moreover (First you work, and *then* you hope you aren't too tired to play.)

their, there, they're

their: (adj.) possessive pronoun form; belonging to them (*Their* vacation begins June 8.)

there: (adv.) at or in that place; also used as an expletive (Be *there* promptly, if possible.)

they're: contracted form of *they + are* (*They're* right here.)

theirs, there's

theirs: possessive form of *they,* used as a pronoun (*Theirs* is the best idea yet.)

there's: contraction of *there is* or *there has* (*There's* been no response to my request as yet.)

threw, through, thorough

threw: (v.) past of *throw* (That answer really *threw* me a curve.)

through: (prep.) by means of; in one side/out the other; (adv.) finished (Did you pass *through* Kentucky on your way to Arizona?)

thorough: (adj.) complete; absolute; painstakingly done (Before you file your tax returns, make sure you've done a *thorough* job with them.)

to, too, two

to: (prep.) toward; on, onto, at; until; etc.; also sign of the infinitive (*to* me, the decision *to* go *to* Las Vegas was unwise, considering his membership in Gamblers Anonymous.)

too: (adv.) more than enough; also (One slot machine offers *too* much temptation to some.)

two: (n., adj.) one plus one (Even a stay of *two* days is too dangerous for someone like him.)

who's, whose

who's: contracted form of *who* + *is* or *who* + *has* (*Who's* your favorite singer?)

whose: (pron.) that or those belonging to whom; also, used as possessive pronoun (These are my keys; *whose* are those?)

wright, write, right, rite

wright: (n.) one who makes or constructs; often in compounded forms (Shakespeare is the greatest English play*wright* of all.)

write: to mark or print words on a surface (Do more people today *write* on computers than with pen and paper?)

right: (adj.) correct; (n.) privilege (It is hard to tell which is *right*.)

rite: (n.) a formal procedure; set of traditional practices; ceremony (The marriage ceremony is a religious *rite* and also a civilly licensed union.)

In the blank spaces, write the correct choice from the words in parentheses.

1. Despite her _____ (loose, lose, loss), the skater showed her _____ (meddle, mettle, metal) throughout the competition.

2. Inside the _____ (envelop, envelope) is the _____ (receipt, recipe) for the payment.

3. The police chief requested more _____ (personal, personnel) for his department.

4. My _____ (advice, advise) is that you should _____ (accept, except) the offer.

5. _____ (Any way, anyway) that you look _____ (their, there, they're) are mountains looming on the horizon.

6. There is not one person _____ (beside, besides) Marcus who wishes to discuss the matter _____ (farther, further).

7. Listen carefully to the _____ (preposition, proposition) and _____ (than, then) decide whether to invest.

8. In spite of her _____ (complements, compliments), Grace's manner caused me to _____ (imply, infer) that she didn't like my menu.

9. A good _____ (conscience, conscious) is often depicted as an angel on someone's shoulder.

10. Before beginning her _____ (prophecy, prophesy), the fortune teller warned us to be absolutely quiet until she was _____ (threw, through, thorough).

11. Nick has _____ (already, all ready) made _____ (a lot, alot, allot) of plans for spending his lottery winnings.

12. _____ (There's, Theirs) nothing wrong with that, _____ (accept, except) that he hasn't actually won anything.

13. If you'll just wait _____ (awhile, a while), I'll serve _____ (desert, dessert).

14. Constitutional guarantees of civil _____ (rights, rites, wrights, writes) should protect anyone _____ (who's, whose) legal residence is the United States.

15. _____ (It's, Its) common for a single actor to have a _____ (dual, duel) role in a Shakespearean play.

16. We sought _____ (explicit, implicit) directions before _____ (preceding, proceeding) into the rugged territory.

17. The deer was _____ (stationary, stationery) for so long that it looked like a statue.

18. The change in plans will have little _____ (affect, effect) on this _____ (faze, phase) of the project.

19. The child memorized the names of all the state _____ (capitals, capitols, Capitols) and loved to recite them, _____ (to, too, two).

20. The ship's full _____ (complement, compliment) prepared for the admiral's arrival.

Answers: 1. loss; mettle 2. envelope; receipt 3. personnel 4. advice; accept 5. Any way; there 6. besides; further 7. proposition; then 8. compliments; infer 9. conscience 10. prophecy; through 11. already; a lot 12. There's; except 13. awhile; dessert 14. rights; whose 15. It's; dual 16. explicit; proceeding 17. stationary 18. effect; phase 19. capitals; too 20. complement

WORKING TO IMPROVE

Most people, including those who know the rules of English usage, hesitate to correct someone who uses words differently from themselves even though they dislike hearing the rules of grammar ignored. This is because they consider it rude to correct someone other than their own children or students for lapses in speaking or manners.

It doesn't seem quite right that if your grammar is not up to standard, you could be the last to hear it.

How to get around this? Choose someone you trust and respect, someone who speaks well, and ask this person to point out the problems you most need to correct. The person will most likely be pleased and think well of you for caring.

Don't try to attack everything all at once, but pick out a few particular problems. Make a point of listening to others and paying attention to the word choices they make. Listen to yourself, too. When you speak, concentrate not just on what you say but how you say it. Check over and revise what you write. Admit to those you respect that you don't mind being corrected—and remember, it's not easy to change speech and language habits you have grown up and lived with all your life. Be patient with yourself.

How you speak depends on many things. It may vary with the occasion, just as you dress up for special occasions and dress down for casual ones. Yet it's important to be aware of the choices you make and the reasons for making those choices. That awareness is the key to putting grammar effectively to work.

Index